ADDICTED TO HER

Janet Nichols Lynch

Holiday House / New York

This is a work of fiction. Names, characters, places, and incidents
are the product of the author's imagination. Any resemblance
to actual events, locales, or persons is coincidental.

Acknowledgments

I would like to thank Coach David Watts and the El Diamante High School
Wrestling Team for their help with wrestling rules, moves, and lingo. I am
also grateful to my nephew Carl Fischer, my first reader, who offered me
valuable insights to the work, especially in the area of Spanish and Latino
culture. Thanks again to my editor Mary Cash and literary agent Jodie
Rhodes; together we make a great team. Finally, I'm grateful for the support of my wonderful family and the camaraderie of my workout buddies
in the Visalia Runners, Visalia Triathlon Club, and Southern Sierra Cyclists.

Library of Congress Cataloging-in-Publication Data
Lynch, Janet Nichols, 1952–
Addicted to her / by Janet Nichols Lynch. — 1st ed.
p. cm.
Summary: After falling obsessively in love, high school wrestler Rafael Montoya
must choose between a reckless young woman and responsibilities
to his family and future.
ISBN 978-0-8234-2186-2 (hardcover)
[1. Love—Fiction. 2. Wrestling—Fiction. 3. High schools—
Fiction. 4. Schools—Fiction. 5. Mexican Americans—Fiction.] I. Title.
PZ7.L9847Ad 2010
[Fic]—dc22
2009029951

To Caitlin

Chapter One

Monique! She's everything I could ever want. The most beautiful girl in the school. Luscious body of a movie star, sun-toasted skin of an Aztec goddess, flashing eyes like meteorites. Making her way into U.S. history class, she wears worn cutoffs with strings dangling down smooth, brown thighs and a pink top budding golden angel's wings, stretched tight over her hot bod.

She hugs Philip. She hugs Matt R. and Matt F. I never got a hug from my darling, but today I leap into line. Her pointy heels click and clack. She hugs Ibraham and Luis. I'm next. Oh baby, come to Rafa.

The bell rings.

Noooooo!

Ms. Becker likes everyone seated, notebooks out, answering the warm-up question on the overhead *before* the bell.

I fling open my arms and *wham!* Monique's tight body melts into my own, which is hard and wiry from wrestling. Her black silky hair brushes my cheek, her soft breasts press against my chest. Is she feeling it? We fit together so fine. I could hold her forever, but too soon there's the release. She offers me her special smile, a chin dip, a single dimple, a glint in the eye as she glides her hand up the back of my buzzed head. It's clear we're meant for each other.

"Monique and Rafa, be seated," commands Ms. Becker.

I feel heat on my nape, creeping up my ears. I wish I didn't get embarrassed so easy, but when a teacher yells at me I'm ashamed. It's how my mom raised me.

Not Monique. She hugs two more boys before ambling slowly down the center aisle toward her seat. Her lower back sort of naturally curves in, making her round ass stick out. When she passes Ernesto, he slaps her with a loud crack. For that, I'd like to drop-kick him.

Ms. Becker looks up from her computer, where she's punching in attendance. "Ernesto! Do not hit girls."

"I didn't hit nobody. Did you see me hit somebody? No, you did not."

Monique's face turns dark and she's rubbing her ass.

"Ernesto, men do not hit women."

He stands up. He's got a shaved head and barbwire tats around his biceps. He could pass for thirty. "Ladies, ladies, she's saying you don't like the way I treat you. Is that right?" He would've said "bitches" if he weren't in a classroom. A good slap on the ass from Ernesto means the girl got noticed. One that hurts says she's hot.

Macho guys like Ernesto treat girls bad, and the girls love them for it. I'm afraid I'll always want to treat girls good and get dumped on.

Ms. Becker begins to write Ernesto a referral to the office, while Monique takes her seat, right next to mine. My eyes wander to her backside, where her white lacy thong slides over the top of her low riders, her sweet little whale tail wagging at me.

A stiff arm passes before my eyes, reminding me to stop staring before I start to drool. It belongs to Victoria Whittle—Tor, she likes to be called now—who sits in front of me. She and I go back to the third grade, when she was the *V* and I was the *R* in the R.A.V.E. Crime Solvers. She's way different now. Tufts of her blond hair are dyed red, purple, and blue, and her black clothes are shredded like she's been attacked by wild animals. She plays cello in the orchestra and electric cello in a metal band—I'm not quite sure how that works. She's a superbrain, and sometimes, when she feels like it, she shifts in her seat during a test so I can see her Scantron.

I'm not much of a student, but I gotta have at least a 2.75 GPA for any hope of a wrestling scholarship. I don't know the answer to the warm-up question. I start copying it off the overhead into my notebook. Sometimes if you look like you're trying, Ms. Becker gives you the five points anyway. You can get through most of school just by copying off the overhead or some smart kid.

My eyes rove toward the profile of Monique, sweeping black lashes, straight nose, puffy bowed lips. I want to say something cool, but I can't think of anything. We've talked some before. I know she likes her Starbucks drink topped with whipped cream because a girl needs a little fat in her diet to keep her skin smooth. She went to elementary and middle schools across town, so she didn't grow up with me like most of the kids in my class, and she even lived in Texas for a while.

"Seen any good movies?" I ask her, but it comes out as a croaky whisper.

"Huh?" She lifts a strand of her hair to peek at me in her sexy little way.

Ms. Becker approaches us. "Monique, please get out your notebook."

"It's in my boyfriend's truck."

Oh, yeah, the boyfriend—Luke Jefferson—a senior when we're just juniors. A hulking white guy, with a truck that could get any girl.

"Can I have a pass to the parking lot?" asks Monique.

Ms. Becker shakes her head. "You know the rules."

"Oh, I like your earrings. Where did you get them?"

"Thanks, but still no pass. Here, let me enable you to learn." Ms. Becker hands Monique a piece of binder paper and a pen.

"Oh, I have a pen." From her mammoth gold bag, Monique extracts a flouncy lavender feather. "I saw you at the Circle R Steak House Saturday, Ms. Becker. Was that your boyfriend you were with? He's hot."

Ms. Becker is short and chubby, and she runs her class like a marine drill sergeant. It's hard to picture her with a hot boyfriend.

"You could go a little lighter on those highlights. I think he'd pay more attention to you instead of doing all that texting at the table."

"You think?" A girlish grin breaks through Ms. Becker's stern mask. Sometimes she crumples into fits of laughter when we least expect it, leaving us to wonder what's so funny.

"Highlights can really rev up your look. Ah! Ah!" Monique crosses her arms over her belly and sets her face on her desk. "Could you write me a pass to the nurse, Ms. Becker? I need something."

"Now, Monique, you can't need something every week of the month. Besides, you should carry it with you. Deal with it between classes."

Monique sits up and announces, "How am I supposed to know when I'll get my period?"

"Count to twenty-eight. And lower your voice."

"I'm going." Monique is quite a match for Ms. Becker. By now most of the students have quit working to watch the two of them spar.

"Leave your phone, then." Ms. Becker extends her hand. That's a tactical error. No teacher is going to get Monique's phone away from her without a huge fight.

"I need it to call my mom to tell her to come get me."

Ms. Becker knows as well as the rest of us that she needs it to text Luke so that he can try to get out of his class, too.

Monique stands, swings her gold bag over her shoulder, and stalks out the door. You can't get in to see the nurse without a pass, so we all have to wait around while Ms. Becker calls campus security to report Monique going AWOL. A lot of school is just waiting around.

Tor turns to me and says, "Why use her period as an excuse? Why not, 'Ms. Becker, I need a pass to go screw my boyfriend?'"

"She could really be sick," I say in a lame defense.

Tor tightens the corners of her small mouth in cynical amusement. "Dude, how gullible are you?"

Ms. Becker finally gets off the phone. She opens her desk drawer, takes out a little hand mirror, and turns to the wall. You can just bet she's considering those highlights.

That afternoon, waiting my turn to pull out of the high school parking lot, I stare straight ahead at the back of the heads of Luke Jefferson and Monique in his silver-and-black monster truck. It's jacked up so high that the axle is exposed like the balls of a prize bull. What would Luke be without that truck? Nothing but a greasy, auto shop guy. He doesn't deserve my angel. I, Rafael Gabriel Javier Montoya, have to find a way to make Monique Cardera mine.

But how? I can't imagine her in my mom's crappy Toyota Camry that's twelve years old, maroon, and has like no power. It beats riding the bus with the other Northside kids, but not by much, and it's not like I can go wherever I want. I run a damn taxi service. In the mornings I drop off my mom at the clinic, Jojo at his middle school, and America at her elementary school. In the afternoons it's the reverse, except by then Jesús is out of bed, and he picks up Mom in his beat-up old van.

Mom is a phlebotomist, someone who draws blood. The clinic people like her because she never misses a vein, and she can deal with the Spanish speakers. She can even get crying kids to chill. Jesús is a nobody who lives with us, an illegal from El Salvador, but he makes my mom happy. Together they made America.

Up ahead, Luke guns his motor, and black soot shoots into the air out of the two huge exhaust pipes on either side of his cab, a modification he probably made in auto shop. I'm not a tree hugger or anything, but we all gotta breathe that crap. He rolls over the curb and plows the grass alongside the line of cars. When he gets to the gate he guns the motor and angles through, knowing the next person in line will brake for him. He lays a patch screeching around the corner, zooming out of sight with my angel.

With a deep sigh, I think how I've got nothing to look forward to. I'll drop Jojo and America home; I'll drive back to school for wrestling practice. When I get home a second time, we'll all sit down to the "healthy meal" my mom has made, which I can only have a taste of because I'm always trying to make weight at a hundred fifty-two pounds. I'll do my homework, then go to bed early so I can get up and do it all over again the next day. Some life.

By the time I get over to the elementary school, just a few kids are left, waiting for their rides. America is seven in the second grade, but already she's leaning backward with the weight of her backpack. Inside it, besides the empty pink Disney princesses lunch box, is a pile of books. She's also reading one, her thumbs pressing down the pages against the wind. Lately she's been working through a series about a kid named Horrible Harry. I know because she follows me around the house reading to me.

She climbs into the front seat and announces, "The moon is not a planet."

"It's not?"

"No." I like the way her hair changes throughout the day. In the morning, when I drop her off, it's in two tight, shiny braids, but now, little wispy hairs have escaped from the braids and are curled around her face like she's been through fire. All day she's been grouping those little colored tiles in math, reading up a storm, and raising her hand about a hundred times. Her wide brown eyes gleam with knowledge. "Wanna know the names of the planets, Rafa? There's Mercury, Venus, Earth, Mars, Jupiter, Saturn, Uranus, and Neptune." She talks so fast, spit flies over her pink gums where her adult teeth are coming in. "Pluto is not a planet."

"It's not?"

"It's just a dirty snowball." She smooths her jumper over her knees. All the other girls wear pants or shorts, of course, but not America. She insists on a jumper and a blouse every day. Mom sews them, and Jesús got a couple of them from El Salvador. "It's called the solar system because all the planets twirl around the sun. Get it? *Sol* means sun, like in Spanish. Why are there Spanish words inside English words, Rafa?"

"Not Spanish. Latin."

"What's Latin?"

"Another language."

"Sounds like Spanish." America's Spanish is as fluent

as her English because she's been talking to Jesús since she was a baby. "Hey, is this Latin the same one that's in Latin America?"

"Dunno. You ask too many questions."

"That's what Mrs. Gunnison says. Know what, Rafa?"

I smooth some of the flying little hairs off her forehead. "What's that, my country?"

"Not too many kids ask questions. Most of them just sit there. Wouldn't that be boring, just sitting there the whole day?"

"Yep." I don't tell her I've been just sitting there my whole life.

We drive over to the middle school and wait in the parking lot for Jojo as the school empties out. Only the kids playing sports out in the fields seem to be left. After-school sports have gotten me out of a lot of work. Jesús is big on education, and anything that has to do with school, he's all for. When I was in middle school I did football in the fall, wrestling in the winter, and baseball in the spring. As a little kid, Jojo was super at soccer, even made the all-city team at ten. But then his grades went into the toilet, and for a punishment, Jesús convinced Mom to ground him from soccer. That was a mistake. I wish Mom would've won out on that one.

Mom and Jesús don't agree on how to deal with Jojo. Jesús is into tough love, and Mom is into baby love. When Mom was pregnant with Jojo, our dad was having an affair, and soon after Jojo was born, he split. As a consolation, Mom would sit and rock and nurse Jojo all day. She said he was a snuggler, not like America, who pressed a fist between her breasts as she ate, eager to be on her way in the world. Jojo is still Mom's baby to this day. Whenever he gets into trouble, she can't stay mad at him for long.

America and I decide to get out of the car and go looking for Jojo. We try the blacktop area, the quad, and the detention room. No sign of him.

I put my hand on top of America's head and steer her toward the car. "Let's go."

"We can't just leave Jojo. How will he get home?"

"That's his problem. I can't be late for wrestling."

Just as we're driving past the 7-Eleven, I spot Jojo and two of his no-good homeboys running along the road. They're quite a sight, each one holding up his monster jeans with one hand and cradling his contraband in the pouch of his hoodie with the other. Jojo's head is shaved on the sides, and his long tail flaps behind him.

I pull over onto the soft shoulder, and America yells out the passenger window, "Jojo, hey, Jojo! Wait!"

His eyes slide toward us, and then he and his hoodlum friends cut across a field and hop over a fence into someone's backyard. A fierce dog barks a warning. I hope it bites Jojo in the ass.

"What's he doing?" asks America.

"Going out for cross-country," I say, trying not to let on to America how really pissed I am. "Hang on, my country." I wait for a break in traffic, pull an illegal U-turn, and head back to the 7-Eleven. "Stay here," I tell her, and enter the store.

The cashier is alone, hunched over a miniature TV.

"Hey, those punks who tore out of here—what'd they jack?'"

"Beer." His lips tighten. "They was looking at the sodas when I started ringing up a guy, and just as I'm getting change out of the register, I seen them slam the beer case shut and hightail it out the door."

"No way," I say, acting like a mildly interested bystander. "What'd ya do about it?"

He shakes his head. "It ain't my beer. I ain't chasing no criminals."

"Did you call the cops?"

"So like a half hour later they show?" The cashier bats the air, his eyes dropping to the TV again.

I turn to leave, but then I see America peering through the windshield. She knows I'm upset, but she can't figure out why. I buy her a small blue raspberry Slurpee.

"How come I get this?" she asks as she takes the cool treat from my hands.

"Reading all those books, you deserve a reward."

"Thanks, but reading is its own reward."

Ha! My little sister talks like a teacher! Maybe how great America is can make up for how rotten Jojo is, but I don't think it works that way.

Chapter Two

A few hours later, I'm hard at it, going one-on-one with Jack Dudley. He's a junior too, bigger and stronger than me, but not as quick and smart, with one ugly cauliflower ear to prove it. He crouches down from neutral position and tries to shoot a double-leg takedown, but I'm ready for him. I sprawl, kicking my legs straight back, and—*boom!*—my chest comes down on his back. I scramble around behind him and pin his legs with mine. Takedown! Now I just need to turn him for the pin.

He's trying to buck me off him. With his back bowed, his butt sort of sticks out, reminding me of Monique, but of course The Dud's ass doesn't look anything like—*wham!* The back of my head smacks the mat, both my shoulders down.

"Pin!" shouts The Dud, his wide, lopsided grin breaking out of his oatmeal face. He's bounding around the mat, smacking high-fives with the air so I have to roll around to dodge his size-thirteen wrestling shoes. Finally he notices me, gives me a hand up, then dashes out of the gym for a drink of water.

Diego Navarro, who's paired up with Andrea Kent in the circle next to us, just shakes his head. He's the captain of the team and has been my best friend since we were in the seventh grade.

"I had him, man," I start explaining. "I don't know how The Dud pulled that escape."

"Who is she?"

Wrestling takes strength and agility, but it's about 99 percent mental. I hate to admit to Diego that I blew it by losing concentration for two seconds, so I play dumb. "I wasn't thinking of any girl."

Diego's eyebrows shoot up like he doesn't believe me. He has a broad nose that's sort of squashed down and his teeth are jacked up, but his looks don't bother him. His chest is broad compared to his short, squat body. The veins pop through his forearms as he places his hands on his hips, waiting for a more accurate response.

"You know Monique Cardera?" I say real low so Andy can't hear.

He snorts. "*Of* her."

"What? You think she's out of my league?"

"I think you're out of hers."

Diego is not a sarcastic guy. It hurts what he said about Monique, even though he means it as a compliment to me. "We talking about the same girl? She's hot."

"Isn't she with that loser Luke Jefferson?"

"Exactly." I'm dying to tell him I hugged her today. I remember her smiling into my eyes and rubbing the back of my head. My arms and chest have been like on fire all day.

"Who are we talking about?" Andy jumps into my circle, crouches down, elbows bent, hands cupped like claws to grab me anywhere she can.

Just when I think I'm in a guy's world, up pops the opposition. "Hey, shrimp. You still hanging around?"

"I'll be in this sport long after you wimp out."

Andy's the only girl on our team. She was the *A* in the R.A.V.E. Crime Solvers when she, Tor, me, and this kid Eric were all best friends. After third grade, Eric moved away and

Andrea skipped a grade, which makes her a senior now, a year ahead of all of us. She and Victoria stopped speaking to each other in middle school, when most girls turn into cute, little giggly things to attract boys, but not the two of them. Victoria became Tor and didn't give a damn what anyone thought of her, scaring off most boys and girls who wanted to be her friend, and Andrea became Andy, quitting childhood gymnastics to take up wrestling.

"There's girls' sports in this school," I taunt Andy. "There's volleyball."

"Men play volleyball."

"Not in this school."

When Andy was in eighth grade and could beat nearly every guy including me, mostly because middle school guys are too embarrassed to wrestle girls, one kid's dad went to the school board to get her knocked off the team. When the ruling went in Andy's favor, it made a big splash in the *Goldhurst Sentinel*, our local newspaper. During high school, when testosterone kicked into every wrestler but Andrea, and a guy broke her arm in a match, it seemed she would quit for sure. But no, that time the paper ran a photo of her training with a cast on.

Now in her crouched position, she starts circling me, staring at me through her wide blue eyes. She's cute enough if you like the all-American preppy look, pearly whites fresh out of braces, honey blond ponytail. Girls have to be small to be competitive in boys' wrestling, and Andy is barely five foot two, with a straight-up-and-down body as solid as a tree trunk. She reaches for my nape, but I duck away from her just in time.

It's tough to be quicker than her. A cocky guy who meets her in a match thinking a girl makes an easy win is in for a big surprise. With her tumbling background and a female's natural flexibility, she's nearly impossible to pin. Before the guy knows it, she's beaten him on points. I'm glad I've grown six weight categories above her now, so I don't have to wrestle her anymore, except like now, when she jumps into my circle uninvited. Lately, the way she's been acting, I'm worried she's beginning to think of me as more than a friend.

I throw down my arms and step out of the circle. "Aren't you supposed to be sparring with Diego? I don't want to have to hurt you."

"Afraid, huh? It must really suck to lose to Dudley."

"Hey, now," says Diego. "The Dud is coming along. I'll bet he gets Most Improved this season." Diego is one of those all-rounders: a B+ student who's in chamber singers, student government, and community service. He could hang with just the in-crowd if he wanted, but he doesn't belong to any particular group. He makes it all look easy, but I know he works hard for everything he gets.

"What were you guys talking about?" asks Andy again.

"Guy stuff," I say. "Things guys talk about with other guys when they're pretty sure there's no chicks around to overhear."

Andy leans forward and looks deep into my eyes like she's trying to climb right through them to get to my brain. "You really think that, Rafa? That there's guy talk and girl talk? Aren't we all just people trying to understand each other?"

"Oh right, and girls talk about football scores and guys talk about what they're going to wear."

"Montoya! Stop talking," barks Coach Folsom. "And that performance you just gave with Dudley was pathetic. Hit the mat. Sixty push-ups."

I do what I'm told, but my face is burning with humiliation. All three of us were talking, but I'm the only one getting punished. Coach is a short, stocky black guy with a ropelike V of muscles across his back from all the wrestling he's done. Obviously he doesn't like me. Blacks and Mexicans don't get along a lot of times, but he never treats Diego like this, and there's slews of Mexican guys in wrestling in California's San Joaquin Valley where we live. He just plain doesn't like me.

Coach stands over me and presses my ass down with his foot. "Good form, Montoya, and when you get done with these, you can do sixty sit-ups, and when you get done with those, you can do two more sets of each."

See what I mean? I'd like to know what I ever did to him.

It's not until later on that night that I get a chance to deal with Jojo. I find him in the room we share, playing video games when he's supposed to be doing homework. I stalk in, rip the controller out of his hands, and haul him out of the chair by his armpits.

"Hey, fool, let go of me." He's a little guy, a head shorter than me, but he's squirrely and strong. With all his kicking and thrashing, it takes me a minute to dash him to the floor.

"Listen, you weenie, I don't care if you screw up your own miserable life, but think about the rest of us. I know it was beer you were packing when you were on the run."

"It wasn't me. It was them other guys."

I press my knee into his back. "What was that?"

"Okay, I had a beer. Big deal. Like you never have?"

"I never stole it, you scumbag. You know you go to jail for that?"

"Like that 7-Eleven fat-ass would bother chasing us?"

I weave my arms through his and clasp my hands at his nape in a full nelson, a hold that's illegal in competition. "You make Mom cry again, and I'll break your neck."

Just in time, I see the doorknob twist, and I spring away from him. He rolls over, sits up, and rubs his neck where I applied the pressure.

Jesús is standing at the door, staring us down with his long, weary face. He's got his own business cleaning office buildings at night, and he's dressed for work in his gray jumpsuit, his name embossed over the top of his pocket. Even pronounced *Hey-zeus* the Spanish way, it's an embarrassment. As if a zillion Marias in this world isn't bad enough—oh, no— some Latinos gotta name their sons after God.

"*¿Rafael, José, qué pasa?*" he asks in his quiet mumble. He won't or can't learn English. Mom, the enabler, talks to him in Spanish and so does America, but me and Jojo don't give in to him. We're American, so we speak American.

"Yeah, *José*," I say, emphasizing the name that he detests. "*¿Qué pasa?* Tell Jesús all about your little adventure this afternoon."

Jojo narrows his eyes at me. "You better not rat on me. I'll—"

Mom's face appears over Jesús' shoulder. She's three inches taller than him, pretty for a mom, with bright brown eyes and wild black hair that she clasps in a barrette at her the back of her neck. She was born and raised in L.A., but after she married my dad, they moved here to Goldhurst, where they could afford a house. When he split, she worked two jobs to keep up the payments. She could do a lot better than Jesús. "What's going on here?"

"Nothin', Mom," says Jojo, flashing her his sweet-little-boy look. "Rafa was just showing me some wrestling moves."

Mom studies him carefully. She knows he's lying, and her tone hardens like steel. "That's enough horseplay. You boys are shaking the whole house. Get to your homework."

Jesús pats her hand and coos, *"Bonita, Bonita,"* which means "pretty" in Spanish. He calls her that all the time, so new people she meets sometimes call her that too, not realizing her real name is Marta. *"Buenas noches, mijos."*

We don't like him calling us that because we're not his sons. He's not even our stepdad because he never married Mom. He's just this guy who showed up at our house about eight years ago and is still hanging around.

"Bye, *Je*sus," says Jojo cheerfully, pronouncing it like God's name, rather than the Spanish way.

Jesús looks sadly at Jojo, knowing he's dissing him, but neither he nor Mom says anything about it.

After they leave, Jojo picks up the controller again, but I yank the cord out of the console.

"What do you think you're doing, fool?"

"This is going to disappear for a while. Stay out of trouble for a week and you might see it again." I wrench the controller out of his hands and begin wrapping the cord around it.

He lunges for it, but I hold it out of his reach. "You're not the boss of me."

"Maybe not, but someone's gotta keep you in line. You can sweet-talk Mom out of anything, and Jesús can't do anything to you."

"The Son of God?"

"*Lamb* of God." I cuff him on the back of the neck, but more like a friend. Together we laugh.

Chapter Three

The next day is Friday, and Monique was tardy for history class, too late to give any hugs. With the final bell at Orange Valley High School come whoops of joy, high fives, and shouts of TGIF. Phones snap open, to text plans for the big game tonight. It's a great moment for everyone but me.

I trudge to the front parking lot, head down, hands deep in my pockets. On Fridays our family's schedule is different. Mom takes the Toyota, dropping each of us kids off at our schools in the morning and picking up America and Jojo in the afternoon. Now Jesús pulls up in his turd-brown van that looks like it's been rolled over a cliff. I climb in, hoping none of the kids I know sees me.

He says, "*Buenas tardes, mijo,*" but I don't say anything back.

I lean against the door and close my eyes. I can feel the van leaving the bumpy roads of Goldhurst and struggling up the on-ramp, onto the smooth pavement of Highway 198. We're headed east of Visalia to Road 152, the site of the Open Air Flea Market, where Jesús rents a spot the size of a parking space for twenty bucks a month—cash. I'm the family member elected as flea market vendor, alongside Jesús.

We leave the freeway too soon, and I pop one eye open, thinking there's a soda in it for me. But no, Jesús is way too cheap for that. I forgot today is shipment day, and we're headed for the Transamer Shipping Office. Every three months Jesús' brother Joaquin sends us merchandise from El Salvador. "Merchandise" is a fancy word for the crap we sell: hair clips, earrings, pottery, shell wind chimes, knitted serapes, ponchos, caps, woven chair hammocks, wooden rosary beads, and carved figurines, all made by destitute Indians living high in the Sierra Madre's with no electricity or running water.

Jesús insists that the flea market is a good way for us to make extra money, but he sends most of the profit back to his huge family in El Salvador.

Squatting on the freeway side of the Visalia airport, Transamer Shipping is nothing more than a couple of trailers on a blacktop area, surrounded by weeds and a barbwire fence. Just by looking at it, no one could tell it's open to the public. Who knows what all comes into this country via Transamer? Every time we come here, I expect it to be closed down. We pull through the gate and park.

Inside the office, a clerk is working the counter. I've never seen him before—a burly white guy in a full black beard, John Deere cap, and lumberjack jacket. He's on the phone, attempting to sweet-talk a woman, in no hurry to help us. Jesús slides his shipping invoice across the counter. Wedging the receiver between his shoulder and ear, the clerk looks over our paperwork, then sizes us up through narrowed slits. After continuing his conversation a bit longer, he hangs up and shuffles behind a flimsy partition.

We wait some more. Jesús rolls his eyes toward me, his face growing long. He always gets worried over nothing.

Finally the bearded guy comes back, wheeling two large cardboard boxes on a dolly. One is crushed in at two corners;

the other is about to explode its overstuffed contents and is reinforced with twine. With a grunt, the clerk lifts them onto the counter. Jesús wraps his short arms around one box, when the clerk says, "Hold on. How do I know you're not smuggling drugs into this country?"

Jesús recognizes the word *drugs*. One time an overzealous Transamer clerk tore a shipment to shreds, and we could only salvage about half the stuff. Jesús shakes his head. "No drugs."

"Let's see your driver's license."

Of course Jesús doesn't have a driver's license. Guys like this clerk can spot an undocumented person a mile away. It's like Jesús is wearing a billboard: ILLEGAL.

"You don't need a driver's license to pick up a shipment," I say.

The clerk nods to the plate glass window, toward Jesús' van. "You need a driver's license to drive that thing."

It's not his job to check our IDs, but we don't want any trouble, either. I take out my wallet and show him my driver's license. "Here, I'm driving."

"Yeah? Well, then, what's he so nervous about?"

By now beads of sweat are popping out of Jesús' forehead.

I try to lift one box off the counter, and the bully places his meaty arm on top of it. "I better hold this shipment for further inspection." Now it's clear what he's after: a bribe.

"I'd like to see the manager," I say.

"I am the manager."

That's probably a lie, but this outfit is so cheap he's probably the only guy on duty. "You the chief of Homeland Security, too?"

"Don't be a smart-ass, kid. Just tell him to pay me a

little surcharge, say fifty bucks, or I'll impound the shipment indefinitely."

"You take American Express? We wouldn't carry any cash into a shady operation like this."

The clerk leers and nods toward Jesús. "All he knows is cash, under the table." He holds out his palm. "Tell him to pay up. I'm letting you guys off easy."

Jesús hasn't been able to follow the conversation, but he understands numbers in English, and he knows what an outstretched palm means. Carefully he sets his box on the floor, wincing because his back aches in a squat position.

I step in front of him, sticking out my pecs, hoping I look like a formidable opponent. "On what grounds can you impound this shipment? Because it's from El Salvador? Because we're brown guys and you're white? Which one of our constitutional rights are you planning to violate?"

The guy tips his beard toward Jesús. "He's got no rights in this country."

"He's in this country, he's got rights."

He squints one eye, looking unsure of himself. "What do you know about it? You in law school?"

"Nope, high school, where you're supposed to learn who has rights and who doesn't. Didn't you make it through?"

"You little jerk. Get the hell out of here before I call security."

There is no security in this place. I grab my box and start backing toward the door before the guy changes his mind. "Come on, Jesús. Let's find a reputable shipping company to do business with next time."

Of course he doesn't understand my words, but he surmises that we're leaving without his having to pay the bribe. Groaning, he wrestles his box to knee level and scrambles gracelessly out the door ahead of me, so that the scumbag behind the counter laughs. Of course we won't be changing shipping companies, despite the shoddy treatment. Most companies don't go high into the mountains of El Salvador where these boxes come from.

After we load them in the van, Jesús climbs into the passenger side and I take the wheel. His thin shoulders are slumped forward and his head is bowed. *"Mijo, mijo,"* he whispers, but it's like I'm the parent and he's the son, helpless without my sticking up for his rights.

I drive us to the flea market. At the gate, I slow to a snail's pace past booths that sell tools, clothes, pottery, jewelry, purses, pirated CDs and DVDs, fishing gear, classic Atari video games that aren't made anymore, and all kinds of fruits and vegetables. There's even a guy who sells live birds. Some of the vendors just scrounge junk at yard sales to sell it for more than they paid for it.

The regulars, mostly poor Latinos like Jesús, hail him with Spanish greetings. Most of the vendors have jobs during the week, probably with managers who boss them around, so the flea market is a kind of working vacation. Later Jesús will wander among the booths to hear all the news and gossip.

My mouth waters with the smells of chilies, Mexican spices, hot greasy corn tortillas, and churros. The flea market can be like a carnival without the rides.

As I back in to our slot, site No. 124, our neighbor Carmen greets us. *"Hola, Jesús. Hola, guapo."* Handsome, she calls me. She's a short, round lady in her thirties, and has a different hairdo every time I see her. Her day job is at a hair salon. Here she hawks purses and wallets, designer knockoffs. Chanel, Dior, Coach, Prada—she carries them all.

Jesús and I set up the canopy that attaches to the side of

the van. The wind is blowing hard, so one corner flaps wildly, and it takes him three tries to secure it. Watching him fumble around, I wonder what my mom ever saw in him.

We arrange our wares on tables and hang some of the chair hammocks and wind chimes. Then we haul two folding chairs out of the van and plop down. The cold wind is pushing rain clouds over us, and I have a feeling not too many customers will be showing up tonight.

Carmen comes over to inspect our new arrivals. She speaks to me in English. Like a lot of people who live in this part of California, including my mom and America, her tongue can switch-hit both languages. "*Guapo,* do I have the girl for you. In the station next to mine at the salon. A very pretty face, but a bit . . ." She extends her hands six inches from her hips.

"How old? How many kids?"

She tilts her head. "Twenty-five. Three."

That forces me to smile, even in my rotten mood.

"An older woman is good, *guapo.* She could teach you things."

Heat scorches my nape. She doesn't mean any harm by embarrassing me, but it just makes me feel worse.

After Carmen leaves, I hunch over and stare at a spot on the asphalt. Jesús nudges my arm so that my elbow slides off my knee. "*¿Qué te pasa?*"

"You know."

"*¿Qué?*"

"I never get to go to the football games like a normal kid. Not ever. I always have to deal with this shit." He doesn't understand every word, but he gets the main idea. He winces at the word *shit* because by using it in this way, he knows I'm being disrespectful.

He reaches in his back pocket and withdraws his ragged

wallet. It's the most painful thing he ever has to do. His hands are small like a woman's, but calloused and scarred. They shake a little as he pries open the wallet and offers me two bucks to buy something to eat.

I appreciate my mom's "healthy meals," but eating at the flea market is a treat. "Not hungry," I say, just to be stubborn. I know I'm acting immature, but I can't help it.

He gives the bills a little shake and nods. I look away, staring into nothing. If I have to suffer, so can he. After a moment, he puts his money away and leaves.

Soon he returns with a steaming bowl of *menudo* and places it into my hands. Two bucks out of his skanky wallet were easy to pass up, but this is impossible. It's a spicy Mexican soup made with tripe, onions, tomatoes, and hominy. My mom does a pretty good job of it, but flea market *menudo* is way better. She says tripe is nasty and uses chuck roast instead.

I greedily spoon the soup into my mouth without even thanking Jesús, but my accepting his offer is *gracias* enough for him. I drink the last of it from the rim of the Styrofoam bowl, some of it dripping down the front of my hoodie. It makes me feel better. I'm beginning to think my life doesn't suck quite so bad when a teen couple walks toward our booth, their arms crossed at their backs, hands shoved into each other's hip pockets.

I scan their faces real quick, hoping they're not kids from my school who would recognize me. Oh crap! It couldn't be worse. I set the soup bowl between my legs and burrow my face deep into my hood, twisting my head so I can spy on them out of lowered lids.

"Why are we stopping here?" asks Luke. He's got thick, dirty blond hair that he slicks straight back to his nape. His stubbly beard grows out much darker and makes me feel wimpy because when I try to grow facial hair it's soft and silky. He's got on tight jeans tucked under his paunch and a jean jacket with a patch on the shoulder of an antique Ford truck that reads Made in America. He tries to herd Monique along with the hand he has stuck in her rear pocket.

"Wait, baby. I wanna look." Her hair is crimped in flowing waves, and she's wearing a fluffy white sweater with a plunging V-neck revealing the rounded tops of her perfect breasts. She reaches for a crocheted *manteleta*, her pink-tipped fingers grasping what I just touched, and drapes it over her shoulder like a blushing señorita. I want to leap up, tie the ends snuggly around her, and drag her off.

Luke yanks the shawl off her and discards it in a wrinkled heap. "You can get all this Mexican crap in Tijuana way cheaper. These wetbacks are just here to rip us off."

"Shut up," says Monique. "They'll hear you."

"So? They all talk Mexican."

"Don't be racist."

"I'm just saying they can't understand us. If Immigration showed up, they'd all split. IRS would be worse. You think any of these guys pay taxes? All they do is mooch off the system."

Luke tosses down a cigarette butt, still smoking. It rolls near our tables, and Jesús reaches out a timid foot to extinguish it. He rises with stooped shoulders and dangles a set of wind chimes in their faces. Monique rears back, shaking her head. Jesús never has any sense of what a customer might want. That's supposed to be my job.

"Hey now, those would look cherry hanging from my rearview mirror," says Luke.

Together they laugh at Jesús' perplexed expression.

"Oh, this is adorable." Monique lifts up a woolen cap, knit in bands of bright rainbow colors, with ties that flutter in the wind. It's handmade and way better than the caps they mass-produce and sell for four times our price at skater stores.

"Come on, bitch. We'll be late for the game."

Monique doesn't seem to mind what he called her, while I squeeze my fists, wishing I could pound him. If she was mine, I would never call her that. Baby, angel, sweetheart— she deserves only sweet talk.

"Try." Jesús holds up a hand mirror for Monique, who arranges the cap over her hair, dips her chin, and smiles at herself.

Luke seizes the cap from behind her and tosses it down. "You know where we are, don't you? It's got fleas!"

"It's sweet! I like it!"

"Let's just do what we came for. If we hit the auto recyclers now, we'll have just enough time to grab a bite before the game."

"Okay," she says reluctantly, gazing fondly at the cap as he leads her away. They get as far as the next booth, and Monique shouts, "Carmen!" She wrenches free of Luke, saying, "Look at your greasy auto parts yourself. I'm checking out these purses."

"If you're not back at the truck in ten minutes, I'm leaving without you. I'm not going to miss the kickoff because of your ass."

"Fine!" Monique tosses the word over her shoulder in a tone opposite of its meaning.

Carmen comes around her table to hug her. "*Chica*, I haven't seen you in ages."

It seems odd that Carmen and Monique would travel in the same circles, but I'm not surprised. People are always running into people they know in Goldhurst; it's got that small-town feel.

"We don't go to Christ Community anymore," says Monique. "Not after, you know, what happened."

"I'm sorry for your trouble, *chica*."

Trouble? The magnificent Monique has problems like everyone else? But she's so beautiful, so confident—how can she? Part of me wants to know the details, yet another part wishes she could remain my perfect fantasy girl forever.

Carmen scowls and stamps her foot. "The little tramp! And employed by the church!"

Monique's face grows dark and she glances down. "Maybe it wasn't so much Ashley's fault. Maybe it was my dad who—"

"Said and done! Water under the bridge!" exclaims Carmen, frantically waving her hand like rushing water. "I hear your mama's remarried! Is she happy?"

Monique nods, smiling. "Very happy."

"And you and big sister? You like new stepdad?"

"Uh, yeah. He's alright."

People never get away from Carmen without telling her what they really feel. "Just alright?"

"You know, newlyweds. Kind of sickening. But after all Mom has been through, she deserves a little happiness."

"That's a sweet girl. You tell her Carmen sends her best wishes." She rubs her hands together in anticipation of doing business. "See anything you like?"

Monique picks up one of the bags with a big pink *C* on it. "Are these real Chanel?"

"For twenty bucks? What do you think, *chica*?"

"It's a good knockoff," she says, examining the inside of the purse. "No one would ever know."

As Monique riffles through her own bag, pulling crumpled bills from various places, Carmen says, "*Chica*, that boy you're with—he doesn't treat you right."

Is it so obvious? I thought it was just me and my jealous rage working overtime.

"He's okay usually. He's just in a hurry to get to the game."

Carmen places a hand on her waist and cocks her opposite hip. "What is it about boys and balls?"

"Oh, I don't know. Where would they be without them?"

"Where would *we* be?" Carmen squeezes her wrist, and they share a good laugh.

As Monique smooths out her money, Carmen leans into her and says, "I have someone way better for you, *chica*. A very sweet boy, *muy guapo*."

"Oh yeah? Like who?" Monique lifts a tuft of hair to peer in the direction Carmen is turning.

I drop my head and bolt like a bullet to skulk among the booths. If Monique found out I'm a flea market flea I would die of the humiliation. I take the long way around the grounds and end up laughing out loud. Me running away from my fantasy girl! And Carmen's description of me did turn Monique's head! Maybe there's hope.

Soon after I return to our booth, the sky lets loose and we're deluged. We pull our tables close to the van and place a tarp over the merchandise.

It's one of those storms that passes over the valley, dumping buckets on everything in a matter of minutes. By the time it's over the customers have vanished. Jesús watches as one vendor after another begins to pack up. Soon we're doing the same, not having made a single sale.

I wait for Jesús to turn his back, then stuff into my hoodie pouch the knitted rainbow cap that once crowned the lovely Monique.

Chapter Four

Finally I get a break. For the first time this school year, I get to go to a football game. Diego has to work, so I go alone. When I get there, I don't see any of the other guys on the wrestling team. Out of desperation, I think to give Andy a thrill and sit with her, but that doesn't work out because she's in pep band. There she is, beating the bass drum with as much enthusiasm as grappling with an opponent on the mat.

I drop by her section of the bleachers while the band is on a break. Pep band members don't wear their marching band uniforms, just school colors. Andy has on a long skinny orange turtleneck sweater and navy ribbons in her honey hair, which curls over her shoulders. It surprises me how good she can look when she fixes herself up.

"Hey, Rafa! You're here!" She jumps up and slings one arm around me, awkwardly hugging me with the bass drum strapped to her.

"Why a drum?" I ask her. "Why not the flute or the clarinet?"

"Are you kidding? When I whack this bad boy, I can feel it in my bones."

"Don't you do anything girls do?"

She throws ice cubes from her empty soda cup at my chest. "You're not really as sexist as you like to come off. You'd have to be a caveman for that. What are you doing after the game?"

"Hanging out at Luigi's Pizza. Diego gets off at ten."

"Hey, that sounds good." Her mouth is open a little, in anticipation of what I'll say next. She fingers the tiny silver wishbone on her necklace, no doubt wishing I'll offer her a ride.

"Cool. Maybe I'll see you over there." I don't want to get her hopes up.

I slink into another part of the bleachers and watch the rest of the game alone, like a dork with no friends.

We lose, 28 to 6.

I'm stuck in a creeping line of cars, heading out the school gates. I text Diego that I'm on my way over to Luigi's, his place of business. He texts back that his shift is nearly done. It cheers me up that we can hang out, but not for long because my curfew is eleven.

A few car lengths ahead of me is Luke's gleaming black-and-silver truck. Luke revs his motor and black soot wafts into the air, tiny specks against the floodlights.

I think of who is sitting next to him, reach into my hoodie pouch, and touch the fuzzy wool cap I stashed there. I drift into a little fantasy of handing it to Monique in history class. "Just thought you might like this," I'd tell her. Then she'd ask how I knew that, and I would tell her, "I always know exactly what you want, my darling." I tie the strings under her chin and she kisses my hand in gratitude, once, twice, three times, little pecks, almost like nibbling on my fingers. She rolls her hungry eyes up to mine. My mouth dips toward hers and—

The guy behind me honks his horn. There's an open space in front of me all the way to the gate. I turn right at the corner, heading toward the intersection just as the light turns green. Blocking my way is Luke's truck, which appears to be stalled. There's a tussle and angry shouting erupting from the cab.

Luke's meaty forearm is wrapped around Monique's head as she tries to squirm toward the passenger door. Monique kicks it open, half slides, half falls out of the high truck, and lands on one foot and one knee.

"Stupid bitch! Get back in the truck!" Luke yells.

"Screw you!" screams Monique. She begins walking down the sidewalk perpendicular to the direction of the truck, looking straight ahead, shoulders heaving.

I hear a car's screeching brakes behind me, and I glance into the rearview mirror, half-expecting to get rammed. The driver lays on his horn.

The light turns yellow. Luke hurls more threats at Monique, peppered with curses. The light turns red. He peels out across the intersection, the mammoth truck fishtailing with its passenger door still gaping, the cross traffic honking.

I wait for an opening, then turn right on red and park alongside the sidewalk. Monique's long, lustrous hair is flying around her head like invisible eggbeaters are at work. Her ass sways in a defiant way.

I roll down my window and call, "Monique! Hey, Monique!"

She keeps strutting along. With the howling wind, I'm not sure she heard me. I leap out of the car and sprint after her, shouting out her name.

She turns and squints in the dark. "Who is it?"

"Rafa."

"Oh! Oh, Rafa!" She dashes toward me and slams into me, her whole body quivering. "Are you in a car?"

"Yeah. Need a ride?" I offer, even though I dread seeing her in our beat-up Camry.

"Yeah, like real bad. I've had it with that asshole. He'll be coming around the block in a minute, and I don't want him to find me."

"Come on."

Monique places her cool hand into mine, and we run like children down the sidewalk. In the car, she twists around, peering toward the direction from which Luke would be barreling down on us. I fumble to get my seat belt fastened.

"What are you waiting for? We gotta get out of here." She hasn't bothered with her seat belt, but bends forward, her head smashed against the glove compartment so she can't be seen.

I finish buckling up. I can't help it. The impulse is too ingrained even if Monique doesn't think it's cool. "Where to?"

"Shelley's. My sister. Get on the freeway, heading east."

Monique stares straight ahead, munching on the inside of her lower lip, quietly sniffling, breaking the silence only to offer directions. It's hard to believe she's truly sitting right next to me in my mom's dumpy Camry, her body like a bundle of electricity charging the whole inside of the car. She has starred in the movie playing in my head for so long.

We arrive at her sister's apartment complex across town, situated in a long row of cheap housing that looks all alike in the dark. Monique uses her own key to let us in through the backdoor. Inside it stinks of garbage, dirty diapers, and stale cigarette smoke. It's dark, except for the flicker of the TV. A warning pulses through my head that my mom wouldn't want me here, but I shove it away. I gotta *live*. I'm so excited and nervous, my legs are shaking.

Two girls are slouched on the sofa, and a baby is asleep on the floor. Monique says hey to the girls. One says hey back, but the other, biting a nail, seems too into her TV show to respond.

As Monique leads me down a dark hall, one of the girls shouts after her, "That's not Luke."

"I never said it was," Monique fires back.

High giggles rise from both girls.

"What do I tell him when he comes banging on the door?"

"Tell him I'm not here."

"He's a brute. He might bust down the door."

When Monique turns her head, I see her smile, and I know the girl is just playing with her. "That's Shelley and her room-mate, Randi."

"Who's the kid?"

"Austin. He's Randi's. She also has a three-year-old girl, Jody, but her babydaddy takes her on weekends." Monique opens a back room and flicks on a lava lamp. There's a desk, a computer, some cardboard files, and a futon, opened up as an unmade bed. "Wait here. I'll be right back."

I wonder where she's going. I look around for a chair, but the only place to sit is the futon, smelling of motor oil, ciga-rettes, and stale sweat. I wonder if this is where Monique and Luke do it. Is that why Shelley was giving her such a hard time?

Be cool, I coach myself. Don't make a mistake and grab for her. Other guys might want just one thing, but I can offer her sympathy and understanding. She might want to cry on my shoulder. I'll hold her without even trying to make a move. She'll see what a good guy I am, that I'm interested in her, not just what I can get. I'll hold her and hold her all night long if necessary, or at least until my curfew, which is in forty minutes.

Monique returns with a longneck beer. "Shelley only let me have one," she apologizes. "We'll have to share."

She switches on a portable CD player, and hip-hop music begins to play, but down low so I can't really make out the words. She sits beside me and offers me the beer. I tilt my head way back, but just take a small sip. I'm not used to drinking because I'm in training.

Monique surprises me. She's dry-eyed and seems to be over all the Luke drama. We talk about kids at school we might both know, the game, and TV shows we like.

"I wish I could get picked for one of those reality TV shows," she says.

"I don't really like them," I admit, forcing myself to be real and not just say what I think she wants to hear. "They're supposed to be spontaneous, but they seem staged and fake."

"So what? I'd make big bucks. I wouldn't have to go to school."

"Don't you want to graduate?" I know I'm coming off like a schoolboy, but I want to know.

"Oh, I'd like to, but I don't see how. I'm way behind in credits."

"What do your parents say?"

She shrugs. "It's not like they can talk. Neither one of them made it through." I must looked shocked, because she rushes into an explanation. "My dad had to drop out to help his mom support his family. Started as a bag boy and worked his way up in the grocery business. Now he's a buyer for a big chain in Texas and makes bank. My mom went back to school later when she knew what she wanted to do."

"Your parents are divorced?" I ask, pretending not to know what I overheard her tell Carmen.

"They tried to patch things up after the accident, tried

hard for two years—AA meetings, family counseling, a new church, but . . . yeah." She nods.

She speaks of "the accident" like I know what she's talking about, so I just nod back. I'm probably coming off as a geek asking too many questions already.

"High school is a waste of time. The teachers are like way too strict. Going pee is our most basic human need, and we have to ask *permission*. You know Lacey in history? She's got a two-year-old, she's a *mom*, and she isn't *allowed* to use her phone during class. I know another girl who's married, she's got a *husband*, and she still has to *report to homeroom*! It's stupid."

"I gotta finish. I need to get a wrestling scholarship."

"For what? College is like more school." She laughs real pretty and takes a long pull on the beer so I get to admire the muscles moving in her throat.

"I don't know what I'd major in. I guess PE." It's a weird conversation we're having. I've never thought through any of this, not even on my own.

"To be a *teacher*? One of *them*? I can't stand them. Like that Ms. Becker. She's so boring."

"Maybe her lectures, but I like it when she goes off on something and is just like talking to us."

Monique tilts her head and mimics Ms. Becker's high-pitched girlish voice, "Education empowers."

The impersonation is so right on I have to laugh.

Monique hands me the beer, and I hold it up to the light. There's like one teaspoon left, and we both laugh. I drink the final few drops and set the bottle at my feet.

She has a faraway look in her eyes. "I've got plans. I'm going to cosmetology school, then I'm blowing this dumpy little town. Moving to L.A. I'm gonna do hair and makeup for the movies."

"That's cool," I say, hoping to sound convincing. How many millions of high school girls dream of making it big in Hollywood?

"I'm real good with hair. It's my talent." She reaches out and squeezes my bicep. Instinctively I flex it to make it stone hard. She's touching me, she's touching me. The hairs rise on my arm. "Wrestling, huh? I bet you're strong."

"Fourth in the state." I don't like to brag, but when I get started, I don't know when to quit. "I could be the state champion next year."

"*The* state champion?" she nearly squeals.

"Well, yeah," I say, fighting for a nonchalant tone. "But there's one in every weight category, you know."

"Oh. How many is that?"

I'm sorry I mentioned it. "Fourteen."

"Oh." A corner of her mouth tightens. She drops her eyes. I'm afraid I've lost her. "It would be cool if you were in football. On varsity."

"I know football gets all the glory. I *was* in football."

"You were?"

"A lineman—just a pawn, really. I played baseball, too, centerfield. Most the time I was just standing around. In wrestling, I'm always on. One-on-one."

"It looks gay."

I stop trying to impress her, and a calm strength sweeps through me. A lot of people don't get wrestling, so why would Monique? I look directly into her face. "Well, it's not. Not at all. It's about power, discipline, aggression. It's about domination."

Her head rears back and her lashes flutter. Her eyes sweep over my whole body and light again on my face. They're different now, wider, deeper. She parts her pretty mouth. She says, "You could make a lot of money, right? You could be one of those cage fighters in Las Vegas."

"That's a horrible thing to say to a wrestler! That has nothing to do with wrestling! Besides, it's the producers who make the big bucks. The monkeys in the cages get peanuts."

"Sor-ry." She holds up both palms. "Can I watch you wrestle sometime?"

She actually means it. "Sure. I'll give you a copy of the schedule."

"Will you show me some wrestling moves now?"

I laugh. It's not something to play around with; it actually hurts, and if you don't know what you're doing, you can get injured. "We don't have a mat."

She pats the futon. "We can use this."

"Too springy." It occurs to me slowly, not because I'm dense, but because I'm so serious about wrestling. She's not interested in wrestling; she's just using it to get something started.

"Then I'll show *you* some moves." She jumps me, knocking me backward. Stradling me, she sits up. Her hair is in her face, one strand stuck to her lips, her enormous eyes peering down at me to be certain I'm watching. Oh, yeah. Slowly she pulls her fluffy white sweater over her head. Her breasts bob in their silky lavender push-up bra. Through pursed lips she breathes the words, "Dominate me, Rafa," all serious, and I have to stifle a laugh. The situation seems to be the exact opposite. I want to shout, "I wanted you from the moment I laid eyes on you!" but I got enough sense to suppress that, too. She collapses on top of me and we're kissing and kissing. If this is a dream, I hope I never wake up.

I start tearing off my clothes. She slips out of her jeans and there it is, a matching lavender thong that I've only seen the tail of. We kiss some more. I unclasp her bra and stare and stare, muttering, "Aw! Aw!" so that she shrieks with giggles. Soon we're naked, lying side by side, the whole lengths of our bodies touching. I'm greedy and want to see all of her. I flip her over, perhaps too roughly, because her voice quivers, half-muffled in the pillow, "Oh! Don't make me go all the way," as if I have control over what's going on.

I'm not exactly a virgin. I know what to do to please her. We touch, caress, explore with our fingers and mouths. Oh my God, she knows what to do, too. She's an expert. We're suspended in time in our own little universe, and I want it to go on forever. My Monique. I have her now, and I'm never letting go.

Afterward, I don't want to move for the rest of my life. Beneath her silky head I cock my wrist to check my watch. Over an hour past my curfew! "I gotta go."

She nestles deeper into my embrace. "You can't spend the night?"

"Noooo." I laugh at the absurdity. "Don't your parents expect you home, too?"

"I stay over at Shelley's a lot. My mom and her new husband *Chad* would be glad if I never entered their love nest."

"They probably like having you around more than you think."

"Oh no, they don't," she says, her mouth twisted in bitterness.

I force myself to stir and begin dressing. Monique, who decides to spend the night at Shelley's, pulls on an oversized T-shirt and red flannel penguin pajama bottoms, which surprises me because I thought every thread she wears would be sexy. When we hug good-bye, the lump of the Salvadoran rainbow-colored knit cap is pressed between us.

Monique pokes the pouch of my hoodie. "What's that?"

"Nothing. My cap." It's *your* cap I want to say. I want to fit it on her head and tie the strings under her chin, and step back to admire how beautiful she looks, but I don't dare. What if she figured out I'm a lowly flea market vendor? "Get ready to be treated right," I tell her.

"Huh?" She looks at me, sort of squinting. She's looking *down.* She's like an inch taller than I am, while Luke towers over her. She doesn't think I'm good enough. I shouldn't have said what I did. I'm way ahead of her in this relationship. She's so used to having Luke Jefferson for a boyfriend, she's probably not ready to move on to another guy, and not so sure she wants that guy to be *me.*

She turns cold and distant. She swings open the door and says, "Bye," with no intention of walking me to the door. I want to make plans to see her, but her face is like a blank wall, impenetrable as rejection. I better take what I got and just leave.

I'm forced to run the gauntlet of the two girls sitting on the couch alone. I wave in their direction, hoping to escape without further derision, but they're not there. In the dim night-light of the stove hood, I see one of them walking barefoot, in shorts, ahead of me. One calf is way skinny, only half the size of the other and sort of twisted. When she takes a step, the heel of the messed-up leg can't stretch to the floor.

Hearing my footsteps, she abruptly whirls around. "What are you looking at?"

There's even more to see. A network of faint scars, like snaking mountain roads on a map, covers the right side of her face above and below the eye. Two words spring to my mind: *the accident.*

She catches me staring again and sneers. "Get what you came for?"

"Are you Shelley?" I ask. "I'm Rafa." I stick out my hand to shake, but she's holding an armful of fast-food wrappings. She sets them on top of the heaping garbage pail, and they fall to the floor. "Shit," she mutters.

"Want me to take out the trash?"

"Would you?" she asks, her voice rising to near excitement.

"No problem." I sink to one knee. "Got another trash bag?"

She hands me one, and I load it up with the overflow in less than a minute. She directs me to the garbage bins behind the carport. I run out, empty the stinking load, then dash back and set the empty container just inside the door. "Good night."

Shelley is still standing there scowling, like she's afraid I'd make off with her trash can. "What's your name again?"

"Rafa."

"Rafa, I think you're nice." She smiles then, looking almost pretty—scars, rotten personality, and all.

When I get home, Mom and Jesús are already in bed asleep, so it's all good. I check Jojo's bed to see if the lump under the covers is really him. He's fast asleep, drool dribbling out of his mouth, where his thumb is stuck in.

Chapter Five

When I wake up the next morning, my first thought is my Monique. Being with her was not a dream. It's real.

My mom calls me to get up. I can hardly move. Last night I was so excited I thought I'd never get to sleep. I snuggle deeper into my pillow, pretending it's Monique, and replay in my mind our hot night together. Oh baby, I've got you in my arms again.

Mom shouts down the hall, "This is the third time, *mijo*. We're all waiting for you at the table."

I look over at the snarl of blankets and sheets on Jojo's bed. Even he's up. I can smell the huevos rancheros, scrambled eggs with tomatoes, onions, cilantro, and roasted chili peppers, wrapped in corn tortillas. My favorite.

I pull on my jeans and a T-shirt and switch on the computer. My stomach is growling, but I can't eat without leaving a good morning message on my sweetie's Facebook wall.

"Rafael Gabriel Javier Montoya!" Mom yells.

All four names go off in my brain like a four-alarm warning. I dash to the kitchen, where everybody is seated at the breakfast table. I hug Mom from behind, clamp Jesús on the shoulder, punch Jojo in the arm, and give America a zerbert on the neck, causing her to squeal.

Mom stares at me like I'm either drunk or crazy. "Did you guys win?"

"Nope." I did, though. I won the hand of the fair maiden Monique.

America is telling a story about some kid who swallowed his pet turtle.

"That's stupid," says Jojo.

"Well, he wanted to see what it was like. He didn't know he would kill it."

I think she's talking about some real kid, but it's in a book she's reading, opened up and facedown on the table to mark her place. To America, the characters in a book are real. It's like she lives inside the book with them.

Jesús doesn't get what she's talking about. He stares into his coffee cup, looking like a hungover drunk. It's not alcohol, but fatigue. He's been up all night cleaning office buildings. With all the work he does, he should make way more money, but the companies whose offices he cleans don't hire him directly. They'd get fined big-time if they got caught hiring an undocumented worker, so they pay a contractor who subcontracts Jesús' cleaning business, and that guy pays Jesús only about half of what he deserves. It's a big ripoff, but it's the American way.

I begin to gobble the delicious food set before me, which tastes even better than usual. America is rattling away to Jesús in Spanish, explaining her book to him, and Jojo is arguing with Mom about whether he can do some damn thing, but I'm not a part of any of it, picturing Monique in her silky lavender push-up bra and matching thong, peering down at me through parted strands of her flowing hair.

I gotta see her ASAP, but I don't have her cell or address. The only way we can communicate is through Facebook. Maybe Mom will lend me the car, and I can go looking for her over at Shelley's place, even though I'm not sure I'd be able to find it. I just gotta get to her, even if it takes me all day to figure out how.

I look down at my plate. The food is gone. I eat America's leftovers and shine both of our plates with two more tortillas from the basket, knowing that all this extra food is going to make my run extra long, but I can't stop myself. I'm hungry, hungry, hungry. For Monique.

Everyone is staring at me.

"¡*Mijo!*" Mom is shouting. "Come down to earth!"

Jojo leers at me. His big teeth are starting to turn yellow with all the smoking he does. "Are you thinkin' of some biatch?"

"Jojo!" Mom slaps his arm. "We do not speak of women using such a foul word." She turns to me. "Jesús has been trying to get your attention. He wants to make sure you remember the job you're helping him with today."

I groan. I did forget. We have to trim all the hedges and trees at this rich dude's house. He's got a huge yard, and hauling off all the trimmings is going to take most of the day.

It isn't until after three that afternoon that I get another chance to go online. I'm tired, sweaty, and dirty. I need a shower real bad, but I gotta get to Monique first. I go to my wall and am disappointed to find nothing from her. I go onto her Facebook to write on her wall. Once I get to the screen with the little box to write the message in, I feel all shy. I'm not sure what to say. I can't just come out and say, "I love you." After thinking a moment, I write, "Last night was real babe."

I think about my message some more. I never talk about stuff I do with girls, except maybe to Diego, and some people reading my message might think "Last night" means we slept together. Luke might get jealous, but then, didn't he and Monique break up? It sure looked like it to me, but then, maybe today he's sorry, and he'll try to make up with her. He'd sure be pissed if he found out she was with another guy last night. He doesn't know where she went—like, she just disappeared into thin air.

I change my message to, "It's real babe." I delete "babe," then put it back in, then take it out again, and fire the message.

I admire my work on Monique's wall. In my profile picture I'm looking all badass. I'm on my toes, my back arched nearly parallel to the matt as I'm flinging my opponent through the air, just seconds before the pin that won me fourth place in the junior state championships last year. Next to my photo is my message, "It's real." It doesn't quite have the impact I was going for, but it gets my point across. The whole world can read it, but only Monique will understand it, and she's all who matters.

I go onto my wall to wait for Monique's reply. There's a post from Diego: "Where were u last night?"

I totally forgot I was on my way to meeting him when I ran into Monique. I write a cryptic message on his wall: "My bad something came up u can guess what." I smile. Only Diego will get what I'm talking about. We have this private joke about that. Then I add, "Meet u at 4," and I sign off.

Coach Folsom expects us to run long on Saturdays. I hit the shower. It's stupid to clean off all the sweat just to get sweaty again, but I'm so filthy from the yard work, I can't even stand myself. I pull on my running gear, then drive out to Rocky Hill, east of Exeter, to meet Diego.

As soon as I see him, I start apologizing. "I swear, man, I totally forgot. Caught up in the moment. You know I wouldn't cut out on you for some girl." That's not exactly true. For Monique, I'd stand up anybody.

"It's cool."

As we start climbing the first major hill of our loop, I tell him the whole story, of course leaving out the details of what happened between me and Monique on the futon. "This is totally unexpected. I was planning on concentrating on wrestling this year. I never thought I'd be going out with someone."

"You're going out?"

"After what we did together last night, I don't see how we're not."

"Lust at first sight?"

"It's love, man. I'm in loooooove." I howl like a wolf. "Oww!"

"Down, boy. She'll play you."

"You don't know that."

"Look at the way she dresses. She falls all over every guy she sees."

"It's just hugs," I counter, but he's got me worried. Does she bring other guys into the futon room? Is that why Shelley got such a big kick out of me showing up there? "Let's just drop it, okay?" A defensive edge cut through my tone, which surprises even me. "You don't even know her."

"I do. Her family went to our church for a while. She's a player, just like her mom."

"Good Christian gossip?"

"It's true! The dad was real nice, everyone liked him. Heading up the youth ministry was this new blond girl, Ashley, fresh out of college, and Monique's dad helped her out a lot. She didn't know nothing, couldn't control the kids. We made her cry once. She didn't last long; don't know what happened to her."

I do. I remember the conversation I overheard between

Carmen and Monique, but I don't interrupt Diego because I want to hear his version of the story.

"Anyways, once Monique's dad was decorating for a dance, and the mom came looking for him. Told him to get his ass home. They had this huge fight right in front of everybody. My mom said their marriage went bad cuz of some accident."

"What accident?"

"Car. One of their kids died, I think. No, wait, she got hurt real bad. Yeah, that's it. Monique's big sister. The mom was drunk driving."

"I met her—Shelley. She's got a messed-up leg and some scars on her face."

"Well, the mom's messed up, too. Been married like three times. Like mother, like daughter, they say. Last night you had a good time with her, so great. Let it go."

His words sting like the wind. I look in the distance up the incline. My calves are already burning from yard work, and we've got eight miles to go. The terrain is all brown, turning bare, dead leaves flying.

When I'm with Jesús, we're mostly silent, partly because of the language barrier, but also because he's a quiet guy. All day I've been sunk deep into my own thoughts. It felt real that me and Monique were together, but now, talking to Diego, I'm not so sure. That's the trouble with telling a single person your personal stuff—that changes it all.

It's quiet for a while, except for the sound of us puffing into the chilly air. Then Diego says, "You mad?"

"No."

"Well, don't be. I'm telling you like it is. That's what friends are for. You better watch your back, *amigo*. Luke looks like a gorilla. When he walks, his knuckles drag on the ground." Diego snorts at his own lame joke.

"Monique practically fell out of that damn truck of his to get away. She could have been hurt—killed—for all that bastard cares about her. It's definitely over, man."

"She told you that?"

"Well . . . no."

"Don't be too sure, then."

There's another long break in the conversation as we crest the hill. It's kind of a shock that Diego doesn't understand my feelings about Monique because he always understands everything about me.

"Andy came by Luigi's last night," he says. "We hung out after my shift, shared a pizza."

"Andy? That new freshman guy on the team?"

"*Andrea.*"

"Oh. Her."

"Why do you say it like that? Inside wrestling practice she's tough, but outside she's all girl."

"Right. I saw her last night at the game, beating the hell out of her drum."

"So? Lots of girls play percussion. Andy's all action, and fit girls are hot."

I guess Diego doesn't get that Andy is interested in me. I know the reason she ended up at Luigi's last night is because I told her I was going to be there, but I don't clue him in. Just because he put down my dream girl doesn't mean I should dash his hopes. "Andy's cute enough. She just gets on my nerves, always pouncing on us guys."

"That would be because her sport is wrestling. What do you want her to do—play Barbies?"

I laugh. "She never played with dolls, even when she was at the age for it. We had this crime-solving club. At recess we would scrounge around the playground picking up

48

trash—'clues'—and then she would make up these incredible mysteries. Even after she skipped a grade she hung out with us, her own age group."

"She told me."

Probably she couldn't stop talking about me. Sorry to be the one to break the heart of my old pal Andy, but once she sees I'm with Monique, she'll have to stop stalking me.

Over the rest of the weekend I check Facebook at least fifty times, but Monique never writes back. I don't see why. I can't believe it's over before it begins, like there's nothing between us. Sometimes parents ground their kids from Facebook; like my mom has done to me, but from what little Monique told me about her parents, they don't seem to care what she does. The only thing I can think is that she's waiting to talk to me at school.

I have an essay to write in English and some math to do, but I can't concentrate so I don't do any of it.

Eleven o'clock Sunday night I check Facebook one more time.

Nothing.

For once, I can't wait to go to school.

Chapter Six

I arrive at Ms. Becker's class early, hoping to have a minute with Monique before the late bell rings. I need an atlas for the warm-up on the overhead, so I go to the back of the room to get one. I turn from the bookshelf the instant Monique bursts into the room, pumping her arms, scrunching her features in a fierce scowl, heading straight for me. I wonder what's wrong. She shoves into me, driving her spiky red nails into my chest, so I have to plant one foot behind me to brace myself.

"Rafa, you fool! Why'd you tell?" she screams into my face.

Tell who? What? I can't think of the words to defend myself. The only person I said anything to was Diego, and he'd never spread rumors.

"He's looking for you, you know. He's going to fight you!"

"Monique! Monique!" Ms. Becker calls from the front of the room, clapping her hands. "Step away from Rafael this instant!"

Monique pays no attention to her. She socks my shoulder—*Ow!*—so I'm knocked sideways. "You think you're funny, Rafa? Wipe that idiotic grin off your face!"

I'm smiling? How could I be smiling? I'm dying. My face must have frozen the moment I saw her walk into the room. I can't move a muscle. I just have to stand there and take it, while Monique glares at me like she hates me, and all the other kids are streaming into the room, clustering around us, laughing and talking smack.

Ms. Becker strides up to Monique and hands her a yellow pass. "Go on to the office. You can cool off there." She makes little shooing motions with her hands, wiggling her fingers toward the door. "Go on, now. Go!"

Monique hunches her shoulders and turns on Ms. Becker. "I am not a dog. Don't treat me like one. Have some respect."

"You have some self-respect," says Ms. Becker in a low, steady voice. "This is a classroom, not an arena for the turmoil of your private life. Please leave."

Monique pans the circle of kids clustered around us. Ernesto holds out his arms to her. She hugs him, the barbwire tats on his biceps bulging. His gaze is tender, almost intimate, which makes me wonder: Has he had a trip to the futon room? No, couldn't be. This time he doesn't smack her ass, but sort of flicks it with his broad hand, like a reassuring pat on the back. On the way to the door, she hugs Philip, then Matt F., her lashes descending upon her cheeks. She just has to get that hugging done. It's who she is and how she gets her power. She reaches out to all the guys but me. I have to straighten out this mess.

My eyes follow her shuffling out of the room, until she slips away from me, around the building. I want to dash after her; I want to explain. No, baby, no. You're wrong about me. What we did together I hold sacred. I would never brag about it.

I notice the atlas in my hand and can't remember how it got there. There's nothing for me to do but find my seat, all eyes on me. After that, the class doesn't get much done.

Ms. Becker is on the phone, calling different numbers in the office, probably Vice Principal Melon, Monique's counselor, the attendance lady, trying to let someone know that Monique is expected in the office. No one seems to answer. When that doesn't work, Ms. Becker starts e-mailing. The class is whipped up, buzzing with the charge of an imminent fight.

Is there really going to be a fight?

I can't believe this is happening. I haven't been in a fight since middle school. It's stupid, immature stuff, something Jojo is always getting suspended for.

When Ms. Becker finally gets the class settled down to start her lecture, one of the campus security guys comes putt-putting up to our classroom in his golf cart, searching for Monique. She never did make it to the office.

I automatically copy the information off the overhead into my notebook. I couldn't say what any of it is; it's just words, letters, chicken scratches. I wonder where Monique went; I wonder who she's with. Did she get back with Luke? Were they ever broken up? Too much happened between Monique and me. If she is back with Luke, her feelings for him can't be the same. I changed them. I know it.

If there's really going to be a fight, it will probably be after school, maybe in the back field that I cross to get to my car in the far lot. Maybe Luke will send me a message through one of his auto shop pals, telling me to meet him at such and such place. Ha! I won't show. I've got nothing to fight about, no reason to sit on the bench the next few wrestling matches.

Finally the period ends. I take about three steps out of Ms. Becker's classroom when Luke jumps me. I expected he would come straight up to me, man-to-man, but he attacks from behind. This makes things easy for me, considering my wrestling training.

I squat down, duck my head, and let him fly over me on his own momentum. He falls like a sack of potatoes. I pounce on him, pinning him with my body weight, while thinking one step ahead of the action and waiting for his reaction. Kids are circling around, hooting for more of a fight, but Luke just lays there, the wind knocked out of him. It seems to be over before it starts.

I let him up, and he rises on all fours, head down, gasping for air. He stands and turns as if he'll walk away, but then he charges me with a head butt to my gut. I tighten my abs just in time to protect myself. Then he holds on to to me, squeezing me hard around the waist. What kind of girlie fighting is this? As I'm working at breaking his hold, he knee jerks me, aiming for my crotch.

That's it. If he wants to fight dirty, I got no mercy. I swing my fist into an uppercut to his chin. His head flings back, his arms flying. He must've bitten his tongue or lip because he's drooling blood. He's flushed in the face and has a surprised, dopey expression that makes me so mad I pop him in the nose.

Monique dashes out into the open from between two buildings, high heels skidding, hair whipping around her head. "Oh, stop them!" she screams, fists flying to her face. She staggers toward us, wringing her white gym T-shirt. "Somebody stop them! They're fighting over me! They could get hurt!"

Someone is getting hurt, but it ain't me.

"Hit him again, Rafa! Hit him again!"

I don't know who's shouting. The whole crowd seems to be cheering for me.

Luke just stands there, his face in his hands, blood gushing from his mouth and nose, streaming between his fingers.

Two campus security guys whine up from opposite directions, pedal to the metal in their golf carts. The first one to arrive leaps out of his cart and restrains my hands behind my back. Luke tries to kick me in the shin, but I dodge him, so that the other security guard takes it in the knee.

Luke and I are loaded into separate golf carts, but just as the security guys are about to drive us to the office, Luke leaps awkwardly from his cart and bolts. From beneath the swaying fringe of my golf cart, I watch Monique rush up to him and press her white T-shirt against his face. He wipes himself off and tosses the T-shirt aside. His burly arm encircles her waist, and together they make a run for it, escaping through the unguarded gates. Soon there's a screech of tires and a blur of black and silver as Luke's truck fishtails into the stream of traffic.

Damn it all. What the hell was that? I look down at my knuckles, bruised and cut from smacking Luke's face around. There's a dull, hollow wind roaring through my brain. Didn't I win? Where's my prize? How did Luke the loser get away with my girl?

Chapter Seven

I'm assigned to in-school suspension for the rest of the day, which means sitting at a desk in the hall outside Vice Principal Melon's office. After a while Coach Folsom drops by.

"What's all this fighting nonsense I heard about?" he asks.

"It wasn't my fault, Coach. Jefferson jumped on my back and I gunnysacked him is all."

Folsom's mahogany face is as still as wood. "You know what this means, Montoya. Next meet you suit up just to sit on the bench."

"Yes sir. I know."

Folsom glares back at me like he expected I would disappoint him. Heat rises to my face, and I drop my eyes to the carpet. He goes into Melon's office and shuts the door. I inch my chair closer to eavesdrop.

"Looks like Luke bit off more than he could chew," says Melon in his deep voice.

"What was it about?" asks Folsom.

"It appears Luke's girlfriend was cheating on him. Rafa is the third party."

"He ought to know better than to mess with another guy's girl."

She was finished with him! I grip the edge of my seat, wishing I had the balls to charge in there and set them straight.

"Who's the girl?" Coach Folsom asks.

"Trouble. Monique Cardera. She's been in and out of this office so many times, she thinks we're on a first-name basis," says Melon.

"What for?"

"A little shoplifting at the Save-A-Lot during off-campus lunch, but that was two years ago after the dad split and she didn't have much. Mainly, she's defiant, dress-coded so many times the office ran out of PE T-shirts to cover her up. We invited Mom in for a conference, and she shows up dressed just like her. I had a hell of time explaining the importance of modesty in an academic setting, trying to avert my eyes from the Grand Canyon." Melon's big belly laugh shakes the door. "Her phone is another problem. It was taken away so many times, Mom got called to pick it up in the office. Within the hour, she barges right in here, yells at the secretaries for being interrupted at work, stalks over to Monique's biology class without obtaining the proper visitor's badge, and hands it back to her with a kiss on the brow."

I grin, just imagining that little scene. So that's it? Monique is superbad for a little cleavage and cell use? I never noticed it before, but she's right. The school is dumb for making such a big deal over such little stuff.

"Well, it's a shame what happened to that family," says Coach Folsom. "I knew the older girl—Shelley—back when I was coaching girls' softball over at the middle school. Lots of spunk. A straight-A student and a hell of a little athlete. She could hustle around those bases, even with that gimpy leg. The dad was there for those girls then, helped out with the team practices—Enrique is his name, Cuban guy in the grocery business—but when he took off, Shelley just stopped caring. Grades slipped to Ds and Fs, never went out for sports in high school."

"I know something about it. Seems Dad couldn't forgive Mom for disfiguring his perfect little girl."

"But he was at fault, too," says Folsom. "The story goes they were both drunk leaving that party, her not as much, so she became the designated driver. I heard he got Jesus after that."

"I heard he got *some*." Melon guffaws over his own dirty joke, and Folsom joins in. "Shelley did graduate, though," continues Melon. "Just barely. Mom was around here a lot, bullying the teachers into passing her."

When I hear Folsom getting ready to leave, I scoot my chair farther from the door, so he won't know I got an earful.

At lunch, Ms. Becker comes by to submit her report of the fight to Mr. Melon. When she sees me sitting in the hall, she starts twisting her hands around like they're under a faucet. "Oh, Rafa, I blame myself for this. I should have had the wherewithal to prevent it."

"It's okay, Ms. Becker. You did your best."

"That's not good enough. Students were injured."

I realize how really young she is. I know she became a teacher right out of college, and this is only her second year. She's not much older than us. "You didn't know when it was going to happen."

"I should have anticipated it. I can't believe it happened right outside my classroom. Are you hurt?"

"Naw. Just my hands." I hold them up for her inspection, and then she says, "Oh dear!" and pats me on the shoulder.

After that, the afternoon is long and boring. An office aide goes around to all my teachers and gets my work. I'm supposed to read three chapters of *The Scarlet Letter* for American lit. I open the book and stare at the words, every once in a while turning a page. I wish I could pay attention to the book and forget about my problems, but it was written a long time ago, and the people talk funny, and it's really hard to understand. If I could get into the story, I might be able to block the horrible thoughts creeping in from the back of my pounding head.

Could Monique have just used me to make Luke jealous? I know what I felt when we were together. It was real. She had to be feeling it, too. Maybe when she saw Luke getting thrashed, her heart went out to him. Monique has a big heart. She felt she had to rescue the underdog.

Another concern: Diego must've talked stuff about me and Monique. It's the only way it could've gotten out to Luke because Diego is the only person I told. He must've said something to someone he trusted, then that guy must've talked. I wonder who it could be. Diego would never mean to betray me, but right now, that's how it feels.

The worst of it is the arbitration meeting later that afternoon. Our school administrators have this stupid idea that if two kids who fight sit down with their parents and Mr. Melon all together, they can talk out their differences and not want to fight anymore. What they don't realize is that kids usually never tell adults what they're really fighting about, especially if the enemy is staring them right in the eyeballs.

On one side of a long oval table sit Luke and his mom, and on the other side are my mom, Jesús, and me. At one end is Mr. Melon and—this is the worst—on the other end is the school secretary, Mrs. Fernandez, acting as interpreter, whom we wouldn't need if Jesús hadn't come to the meeting. Mrs. Fernandez is a short, jolly Mexican lady, all eyeballs and stomach, who refers to Jesús as "Señor Montoya," which is my dad's name, but neither he nor my mom bothers to correct her.

A huge white bandage covers the middle of Luke's face, and he sneaks peeks over the top of it at his mom, who has pinkish orange frizzy hair, reeks of cigarettes, and looks older than my grandma.

She and my mom are both wearing nursing pants and smocks, but Mrs. Jefferson's clothes are plain white and her nameplate says she's an LVN at the Sunnyside Retirement Home, which means she mostly empties bedpans. All the phlebotomists at my mom's clinic wear the same design of smock each day, and today it's pink teddy bears on a lavender background. Mom seems relaxed and attentive, but on her way into the conference room, she squeezed my elbow and flashed me her wait-until-I-get-you-home look. Jesús appears worried as usual, his long face cleanly shaven and his black hair slicked back with water. He's in his best jeans and a plaid shirt with decorative snaps and holds his best cowboy hat in his hands.

After the introductions, Mr. Melon addresses Luke first. "Why the fight?"

"We encourage him at home to defend himself if necessary," Mrs. Jefferson answers for him, pointing a finger at me. "That boy attacked him."

"Just for the record," says Mr. Melon, "witnesses said Luke jumped on Rafa's back as he was exiting a classroom."

Mrs. Jefferson peers at Luke like he told her a different story.

He blushes pink and looks at his lap.

"Lucas certainly wouldn't fight for no reason," she says. "What did this boy do to him?"

No one attempts to answer that. The silence gives Mrs. Fernandez a chance to catch Jesús up on what has been said. Mrs. Jefferson glowers at the Spanish speakers like they shouldn't exist. Jesús seems confused about some minor point, which he asks Mrs. Fernandez to repeat twice, with the Spanish word *espalda,* meaning "back," in it. Each time she says it, Jesús becomes more aggravated.

Melon asks me, "Did you do anything to provoke Luke?"

I shake my head, acting more innocent than I am. "I don't even know him. Coming at me from behind, I didn't even know who jumped me at first."

Luke sets his clenched fists on the table. "You know damn well what this is about. First you get my girl to cheat on me, then you make a fool out of me by posting it all over Facebook."

The heat of embarrassment rushes into my face, and I want to kick myself. How dumb can I get? How could I doubt Diego? It was me who betrayed myself.

"This is about that—" Mrs. Jefferson can't seem to go on. She's pursing her prune lips in a *b,* then opening to a *wh* then hissing out an *s,* searching her vocabulary for the appropriate word to call Monique in a school meeting. Finally she sputters, "that Mexican girl."

Jesús fires rapid Spanish at Mrs. Fernandez, but all I can catch are a few words and *pollo,* the Spanish word for "chicken." My mom snorts out a laugh in a unladylike way, and Mr. Melon, who also understands Spanish, curls his fist in front of his broad chin to hide his smile.

Mrs. Jefferson glares at my mom. "What'd he say?"

My mom shrugs one shoulder, a defiant half-smile on her face.

Mrs. Fernandez chooses her words carefully. "Mr. Montoya wants to know when your son was taught to defend himself at home, was he taught by . . . ." She grins but can't seem to continue.

Mrs. Jefferson raises her voice in announcing, "The official language of the United States of America is English. As a citizen in good standing, I demand to know what is being said here—in English."

"He asked if Luke was taught to fight by your chicken," says Mr. Melon quietly. His face is impassive now, but his barrel chest is shaking with suppressed laughter.

The lines around Mrs. Jefferson's mouth, made by all the drags she's taken over the years, are pressed hard into her face. "We've raised four fine boys, my husband and me. So I guess we've done something right. They all went to Sunday school and they all turned out good, every one of them." She ticks her sons off on her fingers. "The oldest is a police officer like his daddy, the second one is at Fresno State University studying business administration, and the third one, just a young man of eighteen, is fighting for our freedom in Iraq." She looks solemnly around the table, like she expects someone to hand her a medal. "Me and my husband are still in the process of raising Lucas here, the baby, but he's a good boy, too. He's never been in trouble with the law, ever. His daddy would shoot him," she adds in a lame effort to diffuse some of the tension in the room.

"Peeling out of here in his truck with another student when he was supposed to serve in-school suspension is not exactly following the rules," points out Mr. Melon.

"He needed medical attention immediately," blurts Mrs. Jefferson.

"We have a qualified school nurse here." Mr. Melon refers to a paper set before him. "I notice Luke hasn't returned to school after lunch sixteen times this semester alone. He was also tardy or absent for classes on twenty-four other occasions. My suggestion, Mrs. Jefferson, and of course I'm not telling you how to raise your son, is that you take away the keys to that truck for a while."

"That's his transportation. I don't get off work until four."

Melon studies his paper again. "I also see Luke hasn't passed the California High School Exit Exam. We've got classes to help him with that, an hour after school each day. That should fit into your schedule perfectly."

"No, Mom," says Luke, giving her a threatening look.

"Alright, Luke. About today then," says Mr. Melon. "Can you explain why you drove off with Monique?"

"I guess he knows no one around here would treat him fair," interjects Mrs. Jefferson. "I guess he knows you need a Spanish surname for that."

Chapter Eight

There's big fireworks around our house, and it doesn't settle down even at the dinner table. Mom is really angry with me. I'm suspended for two more days, and so are Luke and Monique.

"What was I supposed to do?" I ask her.

"You could've just dumped him on the ground and ended it there."

"I tried to. Then he got up and kicked at my junk."

"Well, you didn't have to hit him so many times." She pats her own nose lightly. "That poor boy's face! You really hurt him."

Jesús places both his hands on either side of his face and says something in Spanish that makes America laugh.

Mom scolds him in Spanish.

I lean my ear close to America's mouth.

"He said that you might have improved that Luke guy's looks."

Mom yells at Jesús some more. They hardly ever argue, at least not in front of us kids, but right now they're really going at it, Mom stamping her feet, Jesús pounding the table so that the dishes jump, both of them ranting a mile a minute in Spanish, while Jojo, America, and I gobble down our chuck roast and potatoes.

A loud banging on the backdoor silences them instantly,

their mouths shaped differently over words they were about to form, their eyes roving toward the door. Jesús' long face stretches longer. His hand shakes.

Any time, any day, this is what he most fears: a rap on the door. ICE—U.S. Immigration and Customs Enforcement—coming to ship him back to El Salvador. You would think government officials wouldn't waste their time with residences, that they would only raid factories, where they can bust hundreds of illegals at once, but these days they're really cracking down.

Mom tilts her head toward their bedroom, and Jesús slinks down the hall. I don't know what he does in there—hides under the bed, in the closet, or in the shower stall? It's futile, he knows. Still, Mom and Jesús go through the motions every time there's an unexpected knock.

Jojo swaggers to the door, his shaved head swinging and rattail swishing.

"Don't let them in," says Mom, the same way she warns us every time this happens. ICE officers can't enter a residence without being invited.

Jojo peeks through the horizontal blind, then opens the door. Three of his homies appear, asking if he can come out. He mumbles something to them, shuts the door, and returns to his dinner.

Mom presses her hand to her throat and shuts her eyes a moment, before she yells down the hall, "Jesús! Okay!"

Sheepishly he returns to the table.

He and Mom resume their argument, haltingly at first, but gradually revving up in speed and volume. Jojo creeps out the backdoor to join his homes while America and I clear the table.

A while later I visit America in her room. She is lying on

her bed, reading a book called *Ramona and Her Father.* Nearly every book she reads these days has the name Ramona in the title.

"What were they saying?" I ask.

She doesn't reply but keeps reading like she's in a really good part of the book.

I sit on her bed, bouncing up and down to get her attention. "America!"

"You should learn Spanish."

"You know I'm taking it at school."

"That's school Spanish. I mean home Spanish."

"I understood some of it, but your dad talks fast in that weird accent of his. What'd he say?"

America rolls her eyes up the page to peer at me over the top of her book. "He's your dad, too."

"You know me and Jojo got a different dad."

"Yeah? Where?"

"Good question."

When we were little, Jojo and I used to go visit my dad for a few weeks in the summer. He lives in his mom's house, where he grew up, in East L.A. He'd take us out somewhere special once or twice, to a Dodgers game or Knott's Berry Farm, but the rest of the time, he'd ignore us. They live in a bad neighborhood with lots of traffic and gangbangers, so we stayed in that hot, dark house all day watching TV and playing a thousand games of Old Maid with Grandma Letty. She was pretty nice to us, but she could get cranky too, thumping us on the head when we put our feet on her worn-out sofa and telling us how happy she would be when we went home.

Some nights after guzzling a six-pack, Dad would start talking about how much he and our mom loved each other.

Soon she would come "crawling back" to him, and we would live as a family again. Doesn't every kid whose parents are split up dream of that? Not me, not anymore. I knew my dad was lying about it even when I was a little kid. How was Mom the one who was supposed to come "crawling back" when he was the one who abandoned us? For years, Mom periodically phoned him to argue with him about granting her a divorce, but he would always refuse. I think he was just being mean. He knew Jesús was living with us and that she wanted to marry him.

Each summer when it got closer to the time we were supposed to go visit my dad, Jojo and I started whining and begging Mom not to make us go. When I turned twelve and Jojo was eight, my mom said we didn't have to since Dad hadn't paid any child support in years.

I don't really miss him. Sometimes I have pretend conversations with him about how good I did in a wrestling match or something, but I would never bother to call him and tell him about it. It's like I don't have a real dad, just a pretend one. The pretend one has my dad's name—Hector—and his macho good looks, but the difference is my pretend dad responds just the way I like him to. He tells me how proud he is of me, how he's going to tell all his brothers and friends about me, and how much he misses me. It's pathetic, I know, but it's better than calling Jesús my dad.

As I'm sitting here thinking about all this stuff, tossing around America's stuffed bunny, she's gone back to her book. I bump her knees, which she's using as a book prop. "Hey, aren't we talking here?"

Her eyes meet mine. "Papá's on your side, you know."

"Yeah? I figured that much, but I want to know his exact words."

"He said you were right to beat that jerk up, that every man must stand up for himself or he isn't a man."

Images rise in my mind of Jesús hiding under the bed when someone knocks on our door, and him shuddering when the Transamer clerk threatened to impound his shipment. "Want me to read to you?"

"No, I want to read to you." I must be making a face because she goes on. "It's a really good book. Ramona's just like me. She's in the second grade."

On the book cover is a drawing of an ugly white girl with a pug nose and freckles. I wonder how she could be anything like America. "Yeah? How?"

"She likes hanging out with her dad. He lost his job, so she gets to spend lots of time with him. I wish Papá would lose his job so he could spend time with me."

I nod, knowing that she hardly ever sees him. I think about the time I spend with Jesús. If it's not at the dinner table with the rest of the family, it's alongside him at work—at the flea market or doing odd jobs. It's never fun, and it's never because I want to be with him.

"His birthday is coming up. I wish I could get something real good. I wish I could get him a green card so he'd never have to hide in the bedroom again."

A green card—a permanent resident card, which would make him legal in this country. Mom and Jesús talk about it so much that America understands that much about it. *Green card* are two of the few English words Jesús knows.

"Do they cost a lot of money?" asks America.

"Probably not a whole lot, but there's lots of paperwork. You'll have to ask Mom about it."

America frowns. "She'll say no. She always says no. She doesn't want Papá to have one."

"Whoa, I don't think that's true."

"What then?'

I shrug, pretending not to know, because I don't want to scare America. If Jesús applies for a green card, there's a chance he'll be deported because he's already here illegally. Neither he nor Mom wants to take the risk.

"I could make him one," America suggests hopefully.

"No, it's not like a birthday card. It wouldn't be the same."

America bolts up to a sitting position and slaps my knee. "Then I could get his van fixed up. You know, a new paint job."

"I think it needs a new engine."

"And a sign! A sign painted on the side that says JESÚS CASTILLO'S OFFICE CLEANING SERVICE. Wouldn't that be cool?"

Jesús would absolutely hate it. He hates any attention drawn to him. It's a good thing America can't afford it. "Hmm, I don't know. How much money do you got?"

"Seventeen dollars and twenty cents. Nearly all my birthday money from Doña." Doña is our mom's mom, who lives in Fresno. She's over fifty, and she's got a boyfriend who's in his forties. She says people calling her "grandma" isn't sexy, so she has all us grandkids—thirteen of them—call her Doña. My mom does too, but only as a joke. Doña's funny, and she's pretty cool, even though we don't see her much. She gives a twenty-dollar bill for each of her grandkids' birthdays, which is quite a lot of money every year when you think about it.

"You should spend your birthday money on yourself," I say.

"I don't need anything. I want to fix up the van for Papá. Wanna chip in?"

"Fo' sure." I reach for my wallet and hand her a five.

"That's all?"

"That's all I can spare." I hardly ever have much money. When I work with Jesús nearly a whole Saturday, all he pays me is a couple of bucks.

"There's more money in there," she says, peering into my wallet. "I bet you just want to spend it on *Monique*." She taunts me by lolling her head and singing out "Monique" on three pitches. I'm surprised she knows her name.

"Who's that?"

"The girl you were fighting over. I bet she has big boobs."

"America!"

"I know you like them. I seen you staring at big ones all the time."

"You do not!"

She cups her hands over her little girl's flat chest and twists her body from side to side.

"America!" I slap her hands down.

She raises her chin to the ceiling and shrieks with laughter. "Then what's so hot about her?"

Monique's hot alright, but that's not what I want to tell America. "Oh, lots of stuff. She's really beautiful and . . . and . . ." It's frustrating to think I'm madly in love with a girl and not able think of a single good thing about her. My reasons are real enough to me, but feelings are sometimes impossible to put into words.

America dips her head and rolls her eyes upward to indicate she's still waiting for my answer.

"Uh . . . well, you'd really like her. She's a lot like you."

"She reads a lot?"

"No! She's a lot of fun."

"What's her favorite book?"

"Look, America. In books you just read about adventures. Monique actually has them."

"What sort of adventures?"

"I don't really know her that good yet," I have to admit, even to myself. I rest my chin on my knuckles and stare at the rug. "I don't know if I'll get the chance now. After the fight, she ran off with that other worthless dude."

"That's messed up! Dint *you* win the fight?"

"That's what I think!" I press my forefinger into my chest. "I just gotta talk some sense into her, soon as we get back in school." I slap my knee. "I'll do it! I'll have a long talk with her and I'll make her see our—I mean, *my*—way of thinking. She's just incredible! I know we were meant for each other! Thanks a lot, my country. You really helped me figure things out."

"I did?" She begins to laugh. She laughs so hard her book slides off her lap onto the floor, causing her to lose her place—the worst thing that can happen to her.

I start to laugh too, not because I have a clue what America is laughing about, but because I got my hopes up about Monique again, and suddenly I'm in a fantastic mood.

America holds her stomach, which no doubt aches from so much laughing. Gasping for breath, she says, "Papá called you a man, Rafa. That's so funny."

It's weird to wake up at nine on a school day, the whole house quiet except for Jesús' snoring. I go out to the kitchen, and there's Mom, lingering over her coffee and last night's *Goldhurst Sentinel*, having already taken Jojo and America to school.

I pour myself a cup of coffee and sit with her. She hardly ever misses work, except when America is sick or Jojo is in trouble. "This is a waste, you know, taking two whole days off. I'd never go running around when I'm suspended."

She lowers her paper to look at me. "I used to be able to trust your judgment, but now I'm not so sure."

It really hurts my pride, her thinking she has to keep an eye on me. When Jojo gets a referral to the vice principal, she goes to school with him the next day and sits by him in every class. "I'm not Jojo."

"Yeah? Make yourself some toast, then get dressed."

"Why?"

"I got an old toothbrush you can use to scrub the mildew out of the shower."

"Mom."

"This afternoon you can change the paper on all the kitchen shelves, and tomorrow, for a special treat, I'll let you outside to rake the leaves."

"Mom!"

"You got your work from every teacher, right? I want to see it when it's done. Then you can read me some of that *Scarlet Letter* book. We gotta keep you busy. Off the damn BookFace."

"Mom." She knows the right name of it. She just likes to annoy me.

Being suspended is the most boring thing there is. Everyone is at school hanging out without me. Even with all the chores Mom gives me and all the homework I have to do, I still have plenty of time to sneak onto Facebook.

Yes, it's addicting. I log on, check my wall, check Monique's wall, check out a few other people. I can't snoop on Luke's profile because he's got it set to private. I log off, and not five minutes go by before I do it all again, over and over. Of course, most everyone is at school, and you're not allowed to use school computers for Facebook. Monique is home and Luke is home, but if they're communicating, it's not online.

The not-knowing torments me. What could Monique be thinking? Does she hate me now? Did she see how dirty Luke fought, what a coward he was? Does our time together mean nothing to her? It's hard to break up with someone, even if you're fighting a lot. Sometimes you gotta break up a couple of times before it's really over.

I could drive myself crazy, with these thoughts going around and around in my head and no chance to talk them over with Monique. Then late Tuesday night the bloody T-shirt shows up on Facebook for an interesting little distraction. After Luke wiped his face on Monique's white gym T-shirt, he threw it on school grounds. Somebody—I think Matt F.— took a picture of it on his cell and posted it.

All day Wednesday I follow the posts of the bloody T-shirt hop. While I'm raking the leaves in the backyard, I sneak through the bathroom window, tiptoe down the hall, and peek at its progress. Later on, I prop my history text open on my desk in case Mom suddenly charges in, while I track the bloody T-shirt.

On Diego's wall, I write, "You guys are making me famous."

He comments, "It's the bloody T-shirt that's famous."

"And everyone knows how it got that way," I comment back.

The bloody T-shirt gets my confidence up. Monique must've seen it, too. She's gotta be impressed. Maybe now she's ready to admit I'm way better than Luke.

Before going to bed Wednesday night, I get up the courage

to leave her a message on Facebook. "Tell me what's going on. Please." I edit the "please" out, then put it back in.

I'm too excited to sleep. I lay awake thinking about seeing Monique in history class tomorrow. What will she be wearing? Maybe she won't bother to show up. Or maybe . . . I squeeze my pillow against my chest and finally drift off, imagining my Monique, melting into me in a long, warm hug.

Chapter Nine

I get to history several minutes early, hoping to talk to Monique before the late bell. I'm sitting at my desk, turned toward the door, when Tor taps me on the elbow. She's wearing her black anarchy shirt and ripped jeans over shredded leggings. She sneers and says, "Where have you been?"

"You know."

"I want that bloody T-shirt."

"I don't got it." I can't tell if she's kidding or not. Would she actually wear it?

"You think it will be available on eBay?" When Tor grins, a dimple appears, reminding me of her younger self, when her hair was as blond as Andy's and the two of them wore matching side ponytails and went trick-or-treating as the Olsen twins from old *Full House* reruns. It's then I notice a round scab above the dimple, dangerously close to her eye.

"What happened to you?"

She points to the wound. "This? Just a little mosh pit accident."

That reminds me her metal band Moldy Muffin had a gig in the Visalia Fox Theatre Saturday, and I was too preoccupied on Monday to ask how it went. "I thought you were onstage."

"I was, but I couldn't resist taking a dive."

"Did your cello survive?"

"Silly! Musical instruments can't leap."

"Didn't your exit kinda interrupt the show?"

"Naw, Muffin Man was taking like a fifteen-minute solo, driving the chicks insane." "Muffin Man" is actually Troy Muffet, a guy at our school who is the leader of Tor's band and plays lead guitar. I've overheard a lot of girls saying he's hot, but the few times I've watched Moldy Muffin perform, Troy's hair flopped over his face, so I don't have a clue what he looks like.

Monique finally makes her entrance in the shortest, tightest black skirt I've ever seen.

"Close your mouth, Rafa," says Tor. "You're drooling on my arm."

I'm not really, of course, but I glance down just to be sure.

Monique hugs Ernesto and Matt F. She hugs Philip and Yasar, a guy she's never hugged before, but he just happened to be in hugging proximity. I want a hug too, but I won't stand in line for it, not after I've had Monique all to myself. I watch her every move, waiting for her to look my way.

She sails toward the front of the room, right up to Ms. Becker. "I'm sorry for disrupting your class the other day, Ms. Becker. I was just so . . . so . . ." Her eyes roll heavenward, in search of a word.

"Distraught?"

"Stressed. I was worried someone was going to get hurt."

"Someone did get hurt. I've changed your seat away from Rafa's, considering the circumstances. Here's where you are now." Ms. Becker walks to the far left corner, first row, first seat.

"Oh, you don't need to do that," says Monique. "Everything is fine now."

It is? What's fine? I want to know.

Monique stands next to her old seat, so close I could reach out and touch her, but still she ignores me. "I can't learn sitting in the front."

From across the room, Ms. Becker taps insistently on the desktop. "Here you go, Monique. Right here."

Monique hesitates a moment longer, then moves to the seat Ms. Becker assigned her. "Fine," she says in a tone that is just the opposite. "Whatever you say, Ms. Becker."

"That's what I thought. Now get out your notebook and begin the warm-up." She stands there until Monique slowly begins to cooperate.

Is she going to ignore me the whole period? I stare and stare at her, willing her to look my way. Finally she turns and smiles at me, her face relaxed and open as if everything is settled between us like the best of friends. Just friends? I need to know what she's thinking. She holds up her pencil and nods toward the pencil sharpener. She gets up and heads toward the pencil sharpener, and I get up and head toward the pencil sharpener, forgetting to take a pencil to sharpen. I imagine my shaky knees buckling so that I'll end up groveling on all fours before her.

I'm so close to Monique, I can smell her spicy perfume, sense the heat of her body, breathe the same air.

"It's cool," she whispers to me over the grind of the sharpener. "It was just one big misunderstanding. Luke thought I was cheating on him with you."

"He thought that?"

"I explained everything to him. How you offered me a ride to Shelley's. That's all."

"That's all?"

"He's fine with you now."

"He's fine?" I search her cheerful, flat face and find nothing in it for me. She steps away, and it's my turn to use the pencil sharpener. I just stand there, a goofy grimace plastered on my face like I need to fart.

This sucks. No, she sucks. I wish I never laid eyes on her.

She's gone, already shimmying into her new seat, taking care that the little tube skirt slides along with her ass and doesn't morph into a belt. There's movement all around me, kids gathering up their stuff. The period is over? I've blacked out for nearly an hour? No, we're headed to the computer lab to do research for our upcoming papers.

Walking across the quad in a cluster of students, I'm as slow and dazed as a zombie. I feel numb, no *dumb*. Like a stupid idiot. Like every kid in this school is watching me, pointing their fingers at me. Rafa thought that lame bloody T-shirt was a big deal. He thought Monique Cardera had the hots for him, but now it's way obvious he's a tool.

Someone knocks into my shoulder. I don't even look over to see who it is. I don't hang out with any of the kids in my history class, so I think it's an accident.

"Hey." Monique bumps my shoulder again.

"Hey."

"You mad at me?" Her smile is slightly crushed on one side, like she might be feeling a little of my pain.

"I'm not mad at anybody." Raging wild animals are tearing up my insides, but I'm not giving her the satisfaction of showing it. I tilt my chin, hold my head up.

Pressing her hip against mine, she searches my eyes for remains of my feelings for her.

I lower my lids, step away from her. "Don't pretend you give a shit about me."

"Who's really pretending here?'

Let her tease. I'm not falling for her act again. I walk faster.

By the time I get to the lab, nearly all the computers are taken. There's never enough for a whole class—ones that aren't jacked up, anyways.

"Double up, some of you," instructs Ms. Becker.

I hate sharing a computer, especially with someone I don't know. I make a dash for the last empty station. I boot up, put in my password, and make it to Google before I see another student squeezing in between me and the kid on my right. One bare leg presses against mine. My eyes have to rove high along her thigh to find any material at all.

"Oh, no, Monique. You're not sitting with Rafa," Ms. Becker shouts across the lab, so all the kids turn to stare at us.

"Got it covered, Ms. B.," says Tor, loping across the room and squeezing in next to me. The school forbids iPods in class, of course, but Tor has hers concealed under her T-shirt and camouflaged in the snarl of wires stuck in her ear piercings, which pass for earrings.

Ms. Becker stands over Monique, making sure she cooperates with the change of seats. She surveys the room and directs her to the far corner. "Lacey, make room for Monique."

Philip raises his hand. Ms. Becker goes to answer his question. Another kid needs help, then another.

Before long, Monique is back, standing over Tor. "Hey, freak, move it."

"Back off, bitch," Tor replies.

"Are you going to let her speak to me that way?" Monique asks me.

Still peering into the computer, I say lightly, "You must like it. Luke does it all the time."

"Rafa," Monique tugs at me with her tone.

Isn't this an interesting development? She wanted nothing to do with me in the classroom, but since I brushed her off on the walk over here, she's all into me again. If that's her game, I'm going to beat her at it using my own tactic: sincerity. "Would you mind, Tor?" I whisper.

"No problem. You two geniuses put your heads together. See what you can come up with."

Monique takes Tor's seat. Soon her knee is pressed against mine.

I return the pressure, furtively run my hand up her smooth calf.

She sighs, lashes fluttering.

"I've been crazy these last two days not being able to talk to you," I whisper.

"Me too."

"You too?"

She lifts a strand of hair to reveal a glint in her eye.

Shit! Nothing but games with this girl. I pitch my knee away from hers. "Don't touch, talk."

"Rafa, I've never met anyone like you."

"But?"

"I've been trying to work things out with Luke."

"What for?"

"I want to want you," she nearly whimpers.

Now I'm more insulted than hopeful. "Like orange juice, just for the vitamin C?"

"I can't explain it, not here." She shifts in her seat to see if Ms. Becker is watching us.

"What's your cell number?"

"Here's something better."

She pushes her thigh against mine.

I place my binder in my lap.

Ms. Becker claps her hands, barrels toward us. "Monique, get away from Rafa this instant!"

I don't know which one of those things Luke found out about—the friendly walking or the more friendly sitting—but after school he meets me head-on in the fire lane, and with one hefty swing, he splits my lower lip against my teeth.

It's a real surprise. I never expected him to face up to me.

I turn and run across the field toward my car before a crowd gathers. It's not that I'm afraid to fight. It's not like I really care if I get suspended again. It's the blood dribbling down the front of my shirt.

If my own bloody T-shirt got posted on Facebook, I'd never live it down.

I've got no energy for wrestling practice a few hours later, but I force myself to show. We roll out the mats, sweep, and mop them. We're about to run the perimeter of the gym a few times while they dry. I try to take off with the rest of my team when Coach Folsom clamps my shoulder, holding me back. His dark face is stern, his bloodshot eyes focused on my lower lip, freshly split and swollen. "This has got to stop."

"It's not my fault. I got jumped—twice."

"It takes two to tangle."

"Today, after school, I was walking down the fire lane toward my car, minding my own business, when Jefferson struts right up to me and socks me in the mouth. I turned and ran like a chicken."

"You did the right thing."

"I wanted to kill him."

"Because you and him like the same girl? What if you did kill him? What next?"

I'd have no competition. I'd have Monique all to myself.

Then I remember all the guys waiting for hugs in Ms. Becker's class, Monique at the head of the line, smiling with open arms. What would it really be like if I snuffed out dopey, doughy, unsuspecting Luke? "I'd go to prison," I admit to Folsom.

"Uh-huh. Waste your whole life. Who would win then?"

"I see what you mean."

He nods. "Civilized human beings do not act on their aggressions in society. Goons, thugs, morons take it to the streets. If you want to punch somebody in the nose, take up boxing, but be prepared to have your own face rearranged. If you want to knock someone down, go out for football. Lots of guys are satisfied just *watching* that, but that's not you, Montoya, right? You're one of the guys who *acts*. You grapple man-to-man. You're a wrestler."

"Yes, sir."

He points a forefinger at my chest. "Stay away from that girl."

If I get another chance with Monique, I'm going to take it. Just because Folsom is my wrestling coach doesn't mean he owns me. Still, I'd like to stay on his good side, so I make an appeal to his sympathy. "She could use a good guy. She's had it rough."

"I know it, but it's not your problem. You've got a big job to do here on the mat. You've got to stay focused right here. Stay away from that girl and that cluck won't come after you."

"Yes sir," I say automatically.

"Say it like you mean it."

I try to glare into the deep, black dots of his pupils, but my eyes skirt away involuntarily.

"Never mind, Montoya," he says gruffly. "I won't force you to lie."

The mats are dry; we're ready for warm-ups. My teammates

stampede around the last corner, Andy at the front of the pack, light on her feet, running on tiptoe. Her pale cheeks are pink with exertion, her blond ponytail already limp with sweat.

She playfully slams into me, but when she looks into my face, her toothy smile fades. "Rafa, what happened to your lip?"

"Like you don't know."

"I don't."

"I ran into a wall."

She blinks hard and her face tightens. I'm sorry I had to dis her, but I'm doing her a favor. Sadie Hawkins is coming up, a dance that gives the girls a chance to invite the guys, and I figure she wants to ask me. I don't want to have to hurt her by turning her down. With the way things went in the computer lab this morning, I still got a chance Monique will invite me.

Diego comes rushing up behind Andy and pushes his palm against her back. She turns to see who it is and laughs. He has saved us both from an awkward moment.

I drag my unwilling sack of bones through our routine. Practice is grueling enough when I'm into it, nearly impossible when I've got no spirit to move me. We warm up with cartwheels, somersaults, crab walks, and army crawls. For the technique segment, we practice reversals. I'm paired up with The Dud again. Every time it's my turn as bottom man, he squashes me like a bug. After the third time, I'm angry and disgusted.

"Sure you haven't gone up two weight classes?" I ask him.

"One fifty-two this morning. On the button."

Over an hour later, as we're rolling up the mats, Diego moves alongside me and asks in a low voice, "What's up with you, Rafa?"

"I don't know. It all seems so pointless."

His eyes drop so that he's addressing my painful lower lip. "I told you she'd play ya, man."

"Not Monique. This."

"What?"

I point to the mat. *"This."* If Monique doesn't respect wrestling, why should it matter to me?

Chapter Ten

The next day, Friday, I look forward to history class more than ever.

I'm disappointed.

I stare at Monique's vacant new desk; I stare at her vacant old one, willing her to magically appear. I twist in my seat for the tenth time, checking the door. Nothing.

Tor smirks at my bulging lower lip. "Why doesn't he beat on her instead? She's the cheater."

"Thanks for yesterday, in the computer lab."

She arches an eyebrow. Actually, hers are shaved off and replaced with drawn-on curlicues. "For coming to your rescue?"

"Not that. For switching places with Monique."

"My dear boy, you're going to have to learn to save yourself. Didn't your mother ever teach you not to play in the lioness's den?"

Ms. Becker stares us down, meaning she's ready to start her lecture. I copy notes off the overhead, my private thoughts rattling on. Monique could be tardy. I can't believe she's sick. Maybe she cut. Damn, why don't I have her cell number?

At lunch, I'm sitting at the table in front of the cafeteria with all the other losers whose moms still pack them a sandwich, carrot sticks, and an apple in a brown bag. One of the guys, Anton, mentions that Monique has been moved to his history class. I don't know if it was Ms. Becker's idea, Coach Folsom's, or Mr. Melon's, but I figure it's to keep Monique and me apart to avoid further conflict between me and Luke. History was the only class I had with Monique, and without that one contact, there's little chance of running into her the whole school day.

I shove the rest of my sandwich into my mouth, then wander through the tables, the cafeteria, and the quad searching for her. I know it's hopeless, that she's off-campus with all the other cool kids, eating at some fast-food place, probably with Luke.

After school, I have flea market duty as usual. I know a lot of people can't eat when they're upset, but for me it's the opposite. I eat a bowl of *menudo,* two tacos, three tamales, and a churro, trying to fill up my hollow spots. I sit in my folding chair, going over in my mind every moment I've spent with Monique. I'd like to talk to Carmen about her, but I don't know what I would say. Her butting in wouldn't help. I stare at the rainbow-colored knit caps displayed before me and stroke the one still jammed in the pouch of my hoodie. I never had the chance or the nerve to give it to Monique.

The whole weekend is as boring as death. I do chores for Jesús. I do homework. I sit around and mope. It doesn't matter if I'm with people or not, I'm alone inside, longing for Monique. Her hair, her skin, her smile, her scent. Waiting to see what she'll do next. The thrill, the flame that torches my mundane, uneventful life. Saturday wears on like a long, miserable run that won't end. I'm stuck inside myself, dying in her absence, with no way to contact her.

I check Facebook. Nothing. I check Monique's profile and stare and stare at the statement, "Monique is in a relationship with Luke Jefferson." It's pointless to leave her a message. She knows I'm here for her. She's got to be the one to act. I return to my wall and post "Rafa misses Monique."

I suffer quietly, alone. Nobody cares. Jojo makes himself scarce, as usual. I wonder if Mom notices how much he's gone. Preoccupied with plans for Jesús' birthday next Thursday, she and America speak in hushed tones and dash out on errands that take all day. Mom has a friend at the clinic whose husband has a friend who does body work for cheap, and she makes arrangements for him to do what he can with the van. Mom and America go to a special craft shop and buy a pan shaped like a football for the cake. I didn't know Jesús even liked American football; I've never seen him watch it. He calls soccer *fútbol*, and I know he likes that, but he works too hard to watch much TV.

I keep eating. Saturday at dinner, Mom stares at me as I reach for my third helping of enchiladas, rice, and beans, but she doesn't say anything. Afterward, I sit around in my room, about to go out of my mind. I wish I could cut out of here, but Mom never lets me have the car unless I have a specific place I'm going to for a good reason. How cool it would be, just once, to drive around, not knowing where I'm headed until I get there.

Diego starts calling me, probably to arrange our Sunday run, but I don't answer my phone. I stare at his three missed calls. It's not like it used to be. He doesn't understand me anymore. I'd like to give him a blow-by-blow account of what went on between Monique and me in the computer lab, evidence that she's falling for me if she can only get free of Luke, but I know Diego would misinterpret things and insist she's merely flirting.

Alone in my room, I find a soft rock station on the radio,

something I never listen to. Then I remember the video games and the controller I took away from Jojo. He hasn't asked for them back, which makes me think he's way too busy getting into trouble. I get them out and start playing, watching myself crash and burn and die, while listening to songs about love gone wrong, somebody wanting somebody he can't have, and this is how I survive my Saturday night.

Sunday morning everyone goes in different directions. Jojo sleeps in, the lazy bum, having crept into our bedroom window as the sky was turning light. Jesús and America go to mass, since he is raising her Catholic. Mom is not religious and goes out to breakfast with her friends from the clinic. I go running at Rocky Hill alone, letting the cold wind pummel my chest, which feels stuffed with straw. I last about two miles. What's the use?

Monday and Tuesday, I search the school and find no sign of Monique. Wednesday, I gaze out the window in American lit and see her far in the distance, scurrying to class after the tardy bell. My heart leaps to my throat, and I want to bolt out of class to chase her. She'd say she's been trying to contact me all this time, that she saw my plea "Rafa misses Monique" on Facebook, that she wants nothing more than to be mine forever. The door of a distant room opens, Monique disappears behind it, and my daydream fades.

After school that afternoon, I pick up America and Jojo, but then when I'm returning to school for wrestling practice, a really weird thing happens. For once, the light in front of the school is green, but I don't turn left to drive through the school gates.

I just keep going straight. I get on the freeway, but I don't know where I'm heading. I might be driving toward Shelley's to see if I can find her place, but that's not it. I pass the city limits. A green highway sign shows how many miles to Lemon Cove and Three Rivers. I smile, thinking of that kind of mad slasher movie where the main character's body is inhabited by a foreign being who makes him do bad stuff he doesn't want to do, like killing a bunch of people, and everyone who knows him is shocked by his behavior, while he's trying to convince them that he's not the one who's doing it.

I don't want to kill anyone; I just feel like driving. I make it all the way up the mountains to Sequoia National Park, but I don't have the twenty bucks to get in. It's no use running away because I don't have the one I want at my side. It's time to turn around.

Driving home in the dark, I'm vaguely satisfied. For once I did something I wanted to do, or anyways what the being inhabiting my body wanted to do.

When I get home and Mom asks how wrestling practice went, I grin and say, "Fine. Good. Really great. What's for dinner? I'm starving."

Chapter Eleven

After school the next day, I'm crossing the field toward my car, my eyes downcast. It's same old, same old. After running a taxi service for America and Jojo, I have to go to wrestling to hear Coach yell at me for missing practice yesterday. Later at dinner, I have to act all happy, celebrating Jesús' birthday and eating the chocolate football cake Mom helped America make. I'm too weary to go through it all.

Monique, it seems, has chosen Luke over me for good, so that's the end of it. I wish I could just cease to exist. Not die. I mean skip over this gut-wrenching hell and move on to a time in my life when I don't ache for Monique anymore, and I can be happy again without her.

I'm sick of feeling this way. I could never tell by the look in her eyes or the way she acted what she really felt for me. That last time we were together was in the computer lab, playing kneesies—what was that all about? "I want to want you." What the hell does that mean? I know I'm better off without her. Why can't I *feel* that?

The grass I'm staring at changes to sidewalk and then to the asphalt of the parking lot. My eyes lift toward fur-cuffed high-heel boots dangling from the hood of my car.

She falls into my arms. "Missed you."

"Missed you." I hold on for dear life. I don't ever want to let go.

"I thought—"

I stop her words with a kiss, a kiss that's like drinking, long and gulping, drowning a thirst that scrapes the walls of my throat.

When we come up for air, she begins again, "I wanted—" and again I stifle her words with a kiss. The last time we were together I was the one who said, "Talk, don't touch," but now it's just the opposite. I don't want to give her a chance to say something I don't want to hear. I don't want her to speak the name Luke. I want to *act*, irrationally if necessary, and fix what's wrong between us later.

I lift her off the hood of the car and set her in the passenger's seat like precious cargo. I dash around the car, jump into the driver's seat, and start the engine.

Monique crinkles her nose. "Is this all you've got to drive?"

I think of her perched high like a queen above the masses in Luke's silver-and-black monster truck. "This's it."

She considers this a moment, then places her hand on my knee and slides it up my thigh. "Let's go."

She doesn't have to say where we're going. I think of America standing in front of her school, growing worried and wondering where I am as more and more kids get picked up. I think of Jojo kicking up dirt and swearing, losing patience and running off with his no-good homies. This is shameful behavior, I know, but my family is going to have to forgive me this one time, because I hardly ever screw up.

"Buckle your seat belt," I say, reaching for mine and looking in the rearview mirror, half expecting to see Luke's truck bearing down on us, spewing black exhaust from the smokestacks on either side of the cab.

Monique drops her chin and peers up at me through her wild black tangles. "I never wear a seat belt."

"You ought to," I say. "Think what happened to Shelley."

"You planning on drunk driving?"

Pulling out into the intersection, I lay a patch with a screech of the brakes, something I never do, but it's just to show her I can. She lurches forward, nearly hitting her head on the windshield.

"Were you in the car?" I ask.

"What?"

"The accident."

"No, I was at a sleepover. My parents only picked up Shelley on their way home that night."

I pull to the curb, stop the car, and buckle her seat belt. "There."

In Shelley's back room, we kiss and pull each other's clothes off in a tangle. Monique leads me to the filthy futon, but I'm not having it and drop her to the floor. This time her bra and matching thong are a kind of shiny fake silk, red as a stop sign. I can hear Mom's lectures in my brain: *Get to know each other first.* I reach into my wallet and pull out the condom, trying to remember how long it's been stashed there. I half expect it to crumble in my hands like dried leaves, but it works just fine.

I speak to my Monique not with words she may not understand but with everything I've got, my mind, my soul, my body. My dear girl, the longer I have known you, the more I have wanted you. What a strange effect you have on me, what power you hold over me. You are always new. I cannot imagine how you will look, how you will act, what you will say next. Always you surprise me.

It is not only your beauty, your breasts, your mouth, face, hair, skin; it's you, the most remarkable woman of all women. Even if you do not love me, I cannot help being utterly devoted to you.

What agony, what anxiety, what torment you have caused me! My mind has been distracted, confused, restless. My wrestling body is well acquainted with aching hunger and raging thirst, but never has it been so deprived as when I first set upon winning the complete pleasure of you.

I know you think you do not need to be loved, that attraction and desire is just a game to play and laugh about, but you do not yet know me, your Rafa, and my power. I will pleasure you, satisfy you, my sweet, incomparable, intoxicating Monique. I will dispel all that is false in you. Your superficialities will fall away like a dead, ugly snake skin, and then only you, the true, the beautiful, the real Monique will be left standing, glowing in the light of your own perfection. People will say, What has happened to Monique? Ha, ha, it's easy. You are loved by me, your Rafa.

After our lovemaking, as I hold her in my arms, she can't stop babbling, "Oh, Rafa, you're so hot. I never realized."

"It's not me, it's you. It's all about you. You make me this way."

"You just dashed me on the floor and took me! You were so into me. Luke has gotten so lazy about—"

"That's over!" I insist fiercely. "You're done with him."

"Yeah, I know. I am, but Luke—"

"Don't mention his name to me! Not ever."

"Well, okay. I'm just saying you're better." She nestles deeper into my arms. "A way better lover."

It's what every guy wants to hear. I'm flattered, thrilled,

relieved even. I look down at her face, checking to see if she's just telling me what I want to hear. She's not. It's real. "It's not a competition. It's because I love you," I blurt, not even realizing the three magic words were waiting on my tongue. "That's the difference. Otherwise, it's no good—empty—just going through the motions."

She lowers her lids. "Hmm, you speak from experience."

"I've had some hookups. Nothing that matters. Nothing like you."

She doesn't tell me she loves me back, I notice, but that's okay. She will.

We cuddle and kiss and talk and touch some more. I could go on like this forever.

Until I happen to notice my watch.

"Shit!" I thought I'd be a half hour late picking up America, not an hour and a half. I bolt to my feet so fast, Monique rolls out of my arms and knocks her head on the floor.

"Ow!"

"Oh! Sorry, sorry. You okay, baby?" I pull my arms through the sleeve of my shirt and rub her head.

"Don't you want to hang out more? I thought we'd get something to eat."

It makes me realize how different our lives are. I'm on a schedule with duties and responsibilities and she's completely on her own, even for meals. "I'm already way late picking up my little sister."

She shrugs. "So? If you don't do it enough times your mom won't be able to depend on you, right? She'll start doing it herself."

I have to laugh. "You make irresponsibility sound like a good thing."

"Works for me." She pulls her top over her head, not bothering with the bra, and flips her hair over her shoulder. "You deserve a little time for yourself, don't you think?"

"I guess."

"You know it. If you spend your whole life doing what other people want you to do, when do you get to do what you want? When you do get any fun at all?"

"I gotta get out of here. You're starting to make sense."

"Of course I make sense. I'm a sensible girl. Hey, you're off one."

I look down at my shirt and see that I buttoned it all crooked, but I can't take time to fix it now. "I don't even have your cell number."

"That's easy," she says.

We take out our phones and program each other's numbers into them. It seems to come late in the relationship. We laugh a little because we're all out of sequence.

"I don't get unlimited service like you," I tell her. "When my quota is up, my phone goes dead, and my mom won't give me more minutes until the next month."

"Some phones are still old-fashioned like that?"

I nod, a little embarrassed. I know my mom gives me cheap service, not only to save money but also the time I'd spend talking and texting. Monique wouldn't understand that any more than she understands the money part of it.

We hug hard one last time. I open the door and pause when I should be dashing down the hall. I don't know how to do it. How do I leave Monique, who is no longer just the girl I love, but a place I live in, and pass into the rest of my life, my family, my duties, school, wrestling, friends, the outside world? Somehow I've got to force myself to do it.

I breathe deeply and step forward.

Chapter Twelve

It's nearly dark with storm clouds. A bitter wind whips the trees. I speed over to the elementary school, knowing it's way too late to pick up America. By now she must've asked to use the office phone to call Mom, who has already picked her up. Am I in trouble now!

I cruise by the school so fast, I almost miss seeing her, huddled against the wind, holding her book close to her face to read in the dim light. She lifts a hand to swipe at her eyes. I've done this to my baby sister, left her all alone, cold and afraid. I'm so ashamed I could die.

I swerve into the circular drive reserved for school buses and fling open the passenger door. America comes running and leaps into the car. She slams her things to the floorboard and wails so loud, people passing on the street could think she's being murdered.

"Calm down. I'm here, now, I'm here."

She only cries harder. She won't even shut the door as the screaming wind swirls through the warm car. When I reach across her to get the door, she socks me on the forearm and shouts, "Bastard! Douche bag! Sack of shit!"

"America!" Of course I know she knows those words, but I've never heard her use them.

"Pineapple penis."

"Hey, take it easy! Where'd you get that one?"

"*¡Cabrón! ¡Puto!*"

"Sorry, my country, sorry, sorry. Look, I'll make it up to you. I'll buy you a Slurpee. Ow!" I rub the knee she's kicked.

"I don't want a damn Slurpee. I'm a Popsicle already. You pig, Rafa. You've ruined everything." She drops her face into her little red hands, her shoulders heaving with her sobs.

"Huh? What?"

"Did you forget? Papá's birthday party! I was going to make paper chains out of the funnies and blow up balloons. It takes me a long time. I hardly have any breath, and I have to stop and wait when I get dizzy."

Somehow I feel less guilty, knowing that she's crying about the party rather than being alone and forgotten in a windstorm. Somehow I feel relief, at least in my own raging conscience.

"No problem. I know just how to make your party better than you ever dreamed."

Less than an hour later I lead America into the yellow kitchen, warm with cooking and rich with the smells of good food. Mom is frying chicken, something she rarely does because baked is healthier and easier, but fried is Jesús' favorite.

"What kept you?" Mom's mouth drops open. "*Mijo,* what is wrong with you?" Monique has changed everything about me, even the way I look. Mom reaches out a cool wrist to test my forehead for fever, but I back away from her, wondering how I smell.

"Nothing's wrong! We've just been running around like crazy." I hold up bags from the craft store of crepe paper, birthday banners, noisemakers, and coned-shaped party hats. America steps around me, a huge bouquet of helium balloons floating behind her.

"Rafa! The expense!"

"It's okay," I say, even though it's not. This crap cost me nearly every dollar I had, money I was hoping to spend on Monique. "I didn't get Jesús a present, and America is so into this party."

"Now I won't have to faint blowing up balloons," says America. Gone are the traces of her tears, although her eyes are overly shiny from crying, which I'm hoping Mom will read as excitement.

"Where's Jojo?" asks Mom.

I shrug. "Don't know. He wasn't out in front of his school when I went to pick him up."

Her lips tighten. "And what about wrestling?"

"Wrestling? Oh! Practice was canceled today."

Mom gives me one of her mom looks that searches deep into my face and makes me flinch. It takes all the willpower I've got not to drop my eyes. Finally she smiles and says, "Great! That worked out perfect."

It's all good, at least for now. America may tell on me later, Jojo may go missing until the wee hours of the morning, Coach may call asking where I was, but for now I'm miraculously in the clear.

After a quick shower, I get busy twisting and taping up the orange and purple crepe-paper streamers, crisscrossing the kitchen. They're ugly, clashing colors, but they're Jesús' favorites. Jojo slinks in the backdoor like a roaming tomcat, just in time to shout, "Surprise!" with us, when Jesús comes shuffling shyly out of the back of the house, dressed for work in his gray jumpsuit. It's no surprise, of course. He'd have to be retarded not to sense something's been going on all week.

After we scarf down the scrumptious chicken, paella, and

chocolate football cake, America hands Jesús the end of a purple ribbon.

"*¿Qué?*" Jesús is wearing one of the cone-shaped party hats, and his expression is goofy with joy.

"*¡Mira, Papá!*" says America, jumping up and down.

"*Un momento,*" says Jesús, then continues in Spanish. "First we must hear Mamá's wonderful news."

"No," says Mom, batting the air. "*Es tu día.*" It's your day.

Jesús sweeps his palm toward Mom. "*Tú primero, Bonita.*"

"Okay." Mom smooths her clothes and beams at us all. "Soon I will return to school to become a registered nurse."

Jesús leads us in applause.

I look at Jojo, and he looks back at me. We are thinking the same thing. How will she pay for it? When will she find the time?

"There is a shortage of nurses at the medical clinic," Mom explains. "The administration offered to sponsor three phlebotomists or lab techs for nursing school. I didn't think I had a chance, but Jesús encouraged me to apply. I won! All my tuition and books will be paid for by the clinic. It will cost us nothing!"

"Mamá is as intelligent as she is beautiful," says Jesús in Spanish, "and she enchants everyone at the clinic."

"That's great," I say, still unsure how she will find the time.

"It is not like regular school. We take sessions instead of semesters. I will be released from the clinic two hours early each day to attend classes, and I must also go eight hours every Saturday. I will also have lots of homework." Mom's hands fly to her face. "Ay, ay, ay! It has been such a long time since I have been a student. I don't know if I can do it."

"You can do it, Mom," says America. With both hands she

pulls Jesús out of his chair to follow his purple ribbon out to the driveway. "*¡Sorpresa!*" she yells. "*¡Sorpresa!*"

Slowly, Jesús circles his trusty old van, running his hands over the surfaces, which have been hammered smooth of dents and freshly painted a vibrant purple. "*¡Estupendo! ¡Extraordinario! ¡Maravilloso!*"

America leaps into his arms and hugs him hard. Over her shoulder, Jesús' eyes pop wide as he stares at the side of the van, painted in bold, orange, block lettering:

JESÚS CASTILLO'S

OFFICE CLEANING SERVICE

(559) 555-1232

His face grows long and grave. His smile slides into the gaping hole of his mouth.

Later on, when I slip away from cleaning up the kitchen to take a leak, I hear Jesús and Mom behind their closed bedroom door, arguing in hushed, fervent Spanish. I don't catch all of it, but I know it's about the new sign on the van.

"Don't worry about it," says Mom. "It's what America wanted for you. I tried to talk her out of it, but she insisted. She's proud of you, and why shouldn't she be? I couldn't turn her down. It will be okay."

"*Ojalá,*" says Jesús. I hope to God.

Just as I get my first chance that night to go on Facebook I get a text from Diego.

"Where were u?"

First I'm benched for fighting, then I cut practice two days in a row without saying anything to Coach. I don't know how he's ever going to forgive me. I text back Diego, "Something came up."

"I hope u no what ur doing."

I know exactly what I'm doing: falling in love. Just as I'm trying to decide if I dare let Diego in on it, Mom barges into the room. I log off Facebook quick, but of course she sees what I'm up to. When she shoos Jojo out of the room, I know I'm in for it.

She sits on my bed, elbows on her knees, and stares at me. "I know practice wasn't canceled."

"Oh. Did Coach call?"

"Nope. You are a lousy liar." She touches her finger beneath my chin to turn my face to meet hers full on. It is a scary thing to look directly into my mom's eyes because there is so much power there. "Your whole life, *mijo*, you have never been able to tell a lie. Your mouth may be false, but your face is always true. You may not like it now, but it's a good thing. You will always be an honest man. You will not even be able to help yourself. Now, tell me. Who is she?"

"Who?"

"*Mijo*, don't play with me. I should know when my own son is in love. The way you've been mooning around here, in a fog, not hearing a thing we say to you, crashing into things—"

"I haven't been crashing into things!"

"You don't notice?"

I have to laugh. "Her name is Monique."

"Is she pretty?"

I smile proudly. "You think I'd go out with a dog?"

"Is she smart?"

I shrug. "Yeah."

"Does she get good grades? Does she read good? Does she have plans for college?"

I sigh in a pissed-off way.

She crosses her arms and looks down at me through her lashes. "I'll bet she has big boobs."

"So that's where America got it! Mom! You discuss my private life with my baby sister?"

"Do you know the difference between love and lust, *mijo*?"

I get tired of these little mom talks. Of course you feel lust for someone you love, but, oh no, in my mom's mind they're completely different. "Course I know," I say.

"Have you taken the time to get to know her?"

"It's kinda new but—"

"Can you be yourself the whole time you're with her? Do you feel comfortable? Accepted for who you are?"

"Well—"

"Then you don't know her." She shakes her finger at me and raises her voice. "You're going to college, *mijo*! Remember? You're going to get a wrestling scholarship and you're going to college."

"That's just a dream that's never going to come true."

"You were a state qualifier! You ranked fourth!"

"That isn't good enough. There's just a few scholarships, for better wrestlers with better grades."

She clicks her tongue and shakes her head. "That's not what you told me last spring."

Last spring . . . it seems like years ago. Last spring I would run two loops of Rocky, lift extra heavy, starve myself—anything to dominate in wrestling! That's all I thought of. Now I don't even care.

"Do you want me to call Coach Folsom tomorrow? Explain about Jesús' party?"

"No! I'll tell him myself." I stare at the floor. "It's just one practice. He'll be okay with it."

She touches my shoulder, as lightly as a butterfly. "And you, *mijo*? You will be okay too?"

"Why wouldn't I be?"

"Don't throw your life away on someone who is not worthy of you."

Like you are? I want to say back, but I know I'd get slapped for it.

"Keep your *pene* in your pants. I am too young to be a grandmother."

"Mom! We haven't even been on one date!"

"This is what worries me." She makes it to the door before delivering her parting shot. "Invite her to dinner sometime. We'd all like to meet her."

Damn! How does she always know everything? I wouldn't want to bring Monique home, and she wouldn't want to come. Monique would have a good laugh at us all, especially Jesús.

My face is burning with shame. This is the happiest day of my life, and Mom had to wreck it. Well, hell. I don't need her approval of the girl I love. Someday she's got to realize I've got a life of my own.

I log on to Facebook quick and edit my profile to read, "Rafael Gabriel Javier Montoya is in a relationship with Monique Cardera." I click on Monique's picture to get to her wall. The computer is slow, lots of kids on Facebook this time of night. God, please don't let it say, "Monique is in a relationship with Luke."

Please don't.

Please don't.

It doesn't.

It says, "Monique is single."

Chapter Thirteen

After allowing America to stand alone in the cold for my own selfish needs, I'm extra careful to always pick her up exactly on time every day. If Jojo isn't waiting for me outside his school, I track him down. One day I chase him across the baseball field, through an opening in the fence, and over Sandy Creek, then take him down as he tries to scuttle up the opposite muddy bank.

"Let go of me, fool." He's heaving and puffing, his young lungs already feeling the effects of cigarettes. "What do you care what I do?"

"A lot, actually, even if you are a little jerk. You're my brother, my mother's son, and she cries easy."

Jojo yanks the cloth of his shirt out of my hand, but walks begrudgingly beside me, back across the field. "What are you talking about? Mom doesn't cry."

"Only about you. You're her one misery."

"She'll be rid of me soon as I turn eighteen. You'll all see my back then. For good. This whole family sucks."

"You suck. And five years is a long time for a punk like you."

When we get home, I do what homework I can and listen to America read to me. Then at 4:45, same as always, I head out again. But not to wrestling.

Me and Monique hang out at different places. The park, the mall, Starbucks, and, of course, Shelley's to fool around. That's where I make Monique update her Facebook profile. With my arms wrapped tightly around her from behind, she types the words, *Monique is in a relationship with Rafa.*

Yes!

Sometimes we just hang out with Shelley. Even though Monique and Shelley have the same mother and father, they don't look much like sisters. Shelley is light-skinned with Latino features, like the stars in the *telenovelas* she watches on the Spanish channel. Monique is darker, with flashing black eyes and the blackest black hair, which she never tints or streaks like other girls.

Supposedly Shelley is going to Goldhurst Community College, but she always seems to be at the apartment, parked in front of the TV. I ask her when her classes are, and she says, "In college you don't really have to, like, go to class. There's no, like, attendance lady calling your parents saying you ditched."

"Don't you have to go to, like, learn?" I ask.

She jerks her head to glare at me with one cold, flat eye. "I don't need to know crap like music appreciation. I just need the GE credits."

"Oh." I wonder how many of those she's earned, but I bet it's not very many. She's in her third year at a two-year college. I don't ask because I don't want to make enemies with her. I'm still not all that comfortable with her because when I face her, she asks, "What are you looking at?" and when I avert my eyes it seems like I'm acting like her scars are too horrible to look at. I get around it by tidying up while we talk to her. This scores points; she likes having me for a maid.

Shelley and Monique seem to bond over ragging on their mom's various boyfriends and husbands.

"You should've met Ottooooo," says Monique, as I collect dirty mugs and cereal bowls with curdling milk from the coffee table.

"Rebound man," Shelley calls him.

Monique fills me in. "Dad left Mom for someone young enough to be his daughter, so Mom right away had to prove she could get someone to marry her, too."

At the mention of their dad, Shelley shoots Monique with her single-eyed glare. "She wasn't that young."

"Ashley's only nine years older than you." Monique hands me the box she's been eating leftover pizza from. "Otto was real sweet to us until Mom married him. Then he was all, 'I don't want to hear another peep out of you,' and 'I can backhand that smirk off your face.' Mom didn't like how he treated us, so one night when he was out bowling, we just packed up all the stuff we could and left."

"She should have taken him to the cleaners," says Shelley.

"Mom always says, 'I got out with my girls and my sanity. That's enough for me.'"

"After that was our best time together," says Shelley. "I mean, we were poor because Mom had gone back to school, and we lived in a crappy apartment, but we were close. For a while Mom didn't care about men. I mean, she still went out and had a good time, but she didn't take any one guy seriously. She'd come home from an evening out, make us clam dip, and we'd sit around eating chips, making fun of her date, and laughing."

"That *was* fun! Then Chad came along." When Monique scowls, she looks more like her sister.

"At first she dissed him, too," says Shelley. "Then he bought her the Lexus."

"That wasn't it! He wanted her. He really wanted her. He still wants her," insists Monique.

Shelley nods. "Yeah. He's all into her, and that's what Mom needs."

Monique raises one side of her upper lip. "Old people having sex—that is so gross."

"I think it's sweet," says Shelley. "Like, we might get old someday, too."

Shelley's okay. Sometimes she can be really funny, without even meaning to be.

On the day we decide to go miniature golfing at Adventure Park, Monique asks me to drive by her house to get a jacket. It's in a fancy new subdivision, Golden Oak Ranch, with only a few streets of completed homes and many lots for sale. At the entrance a billboard reads NO DOWN PAYMENT! SUBPRIME LOANS! INTEREST-FREE MORTGAGE FOR A YEAR! I've overheard my mom and her friends talk about this kind of deal, which makes it really easy to move into a big, new house, but my mom just shakes her head and says, "You gotta pay up eventually."

Monique directs me to her house, which is huge, with towering pillars on either side of the broad front door. Centered in a stone courtyard is a brass fountain of a little boy pissing into a pool of water. I park on the street. The driveway is filled with the shiny black Lexus Shelley was talking about and a classic red Thunderbird.

"Wow! What do your mom and stepdad do? Sell drugs?"

Monique bats my arm, but she's laughing. "Chad sells

insurance, and Mom works at a loan agency that gets poor, elderly homeowners to sell back their homes bit by bit, so they don't have to move out and can still have some cash to live on."

"That sounds nice."

"Not really. The homes are worth a lot more than the people sell them for, and it pisses off their kids because they'll have no inheritance, but Mom makes bank!"

I nod toward the driveway. "Which one do you drive?"

"Ha! They don't let me drive, not after I wrecked two cars in one weekend."

"Two?"

"I was just learning! And besides, one wasn't even my fault. This old guy just wouldn't get out of my way."

"Ha!" I pat the steering wheel. "At least my mom lets me use her car."

"This heap?"

"Better than nothing," we say in unison.

I reach for my door, but Monique has already jumped out of the car. "Wait here. I'll be right back."

It makes me feel like I'm not good enough to be invited in. While Monique walks up to the front door, some little dogs inside the house start yapping, high-pitched and piercing, like there's a whole pack of them. She enters the house, and then I have to wait and wait. A security guard drives by slowly and peers into my car, like I'm a suspicious person.

Finally the front door opens, and Monique storms out, shouting angrily back into the house. Her stepdad is yelling at her, but with all the yapping, I can't hear what the problem is. When Monique's mom joins in the fighting, Monique slams the door on them both.

She stalks down the walkway, flops into the car, and glares back at the house. I don't ask. I figure if she wants to talk about it, she will.

She doesn't.

As we pull away from the curb, I say, "That's some house."

"Yeah, but the people in it suck."

Everyone knows you get away with stuff for only so long, and then it eventually catches up with you. Two weeks fly by, and when a hall pass comes my way in American lit with Coach Folsom's name on it, I know it's my day of reckoning.

When I walk into his office, he motions for me to sit. "So that's it then? You just stop coming to practice? You think that's the right way to end things?"

"I didn't exactly plan it. It just happened that way."

"It did?" He squints one eye at me and cocks his head.

"Well, yeah. One day I didn't feel like it and another day I had this family thing to go to, and, well, I know how strict you are about missing practice. I figured you'd kicked me off the team already, so what was the point coming around to hear about it?"

"The point? Well, let's see. Common courtesy, for one thing. Respect. Thinking about your team before yourself. Now what are we going to do for the one-hundred-fifty-two-pound category?"

"You've got three other wrestlers!"

"I'm talking about a man who can win."

I don't know what to say. The more I hang out with Monique, the more I want to be with her. Winning a state championship seems like a distant daydream, and getting a scholarship even more unlikely. I never even thought about my team, so I say nothing.

He waits a long moment. "Haven't got a thing to say for yourself, Montoya?"

"Sorry, Coach. My heart just isn't in it anymore."

He leans across his desk on his elbows. "Tell me something. Why did you get into wrestling in the first place?"

I shrug. "Because football got boring. Because I had to do some sport to get out of all the work Jesús lines up for me. Because my mom's always talking about me getting a scholarship."

"You never wanted it for yourself?"

I throw up my arms. "I don't know."

"What does your mom say about you quitting?"

I shrug again. "She's okay with it."

Coach considers this a moment, his ebony face as still as petrified wood. "You're a lousy liar, Montoya. Anyone ever tell you that?"

Chapter Fourteen

It's Friday after school, but I don't have flea market duty because there's a two-day wrestling invitational that my mom thinks I'm in. As the bus transports the wrestling team to Yokohl Valley High in Exeter, two towns over, I'm hanging out with Monique at the mall. I've got it set up so Diego will text me the second the bus rolls back into our school parking lot, about eleven o'clock tonight, so that I can walk through my backdoor exactly fifteen minutes afterward. The same goes for tomorrow, which gives me about twelve precious hours with Monique tomorrow, a whole Saturday. I never realized how much time I wasted on wrestling, when I could be out, doing whatever I want.

I take Monique to an early show at the mall theater, and then she wants dinner. I'm afraid to tell her I spent the last of my money on the movie and popcorn, so I make a joke of pulling out the lining of my front pockets.

She doesn't laugh, but she's not mad either. "I know. Let's go to my house. We can raid the refrigerator, if you don't mind leftovers."

"Leftovers are cool." I imagine takeout from restaurants— fried chicken, pizza, chow mein—stuff I wouldn't find in my own refrigerator. "Would your parents mind?"

"Mom and Chad aren't home."

But when we drive up to the house, she wrinkles her nose

at the cherry red Thunderbird and gleaming black Lexus in the driveway. "Crap, they are here. I thought they had some dog show thing."

"Should we leave?"

"No, we gotta eat. Come on."

As we walk through the courtyard, the dogs inside the house start yapping. I get a closer look at the peeing boy fountain. "Man, that's just weird."

"It's art."

"Right."

"No, really. It's a replica of a famous statue in Brussels, *Mannekin Pis*. The legend goes that he saved his whole village from burning by peeing on a fire."

I check her face to be sure she's not joking. Sometimes I just don't know how to take her.

She opens the door and shouts, "Babies! Babies!" Two Chihuahuas glare at me, their eyes bulging like marbles. They step backward, yapping their heads off, baring spiky little teeth, their nails click-clacking on the tile entryway. Worse than that, they've got clothes on. One is wearing a sequined red bra with black fringe tassels, a black leather miniskirt, and fishnet stockings. The other one has baggy purple silk trousers and a wide-brimmed orange velvet hat with a feather plume.

"A pimp and his hooker," squeals Monique. She squats down to let the hooker leap into her arms and lick her face. "How adorable."

"Well, they didn't win," says Monique's mom from the kitchen. "Batman and Robin won. The judges obviously didn't know quality of breed."

"A boxer and a Mexican hairless," says Chad. "Absolutely disgusting-looking things."

The spacious living room has white walls and a white

shag carpet with a few brown spots on it. The only furniture is a deluxe pinball machine and a white baby grand piano. Over the four-foot-high fireplace is a huge oil painting of one of the dogs, probably the hooker, because it's dressed in a pink tutu. If I had daughters like Shelley and Monique, I'd have their portraits up there.

Chad is a white dude with a pencil-thin mustache and crew cut, dressed in a pink dress shirt and purple paisley tie. He's skinny, except for a bowling-ball gut. He looks me over and says, "You're not Luke."

"Chad!" exclaims Monique.

He laughs. "She just loves to torment that poor guy."

Monique sets her mouth and gives her head a short, tight shake to indicate to me that it's not true. Chad must not be up on the latest, but Monique doesn't bother to set him straight. I wait a few moments for her to introduce me, then say, "I'm Rafa." I extend my hand over the kitchen counter and shake with Chad.

"I'm Krystal," says Monique's mom. I'd be more comfortable calling her Mrs. Something, but she doesn't mention her new married name. She's an older, plumper version of Monique in a push-up bra, plunging neckline, tons of makeup, and big gold jewelry.

"What smells so good?" asks Monique.

"We're broiling steaks, but there's only two," says Krystal. "Sorry, sweetie. There might be some extra salad. Is there, Biggie?"

"Salad!" exclaims Monique. "We don't want no rabbit food. We're starving."

"We didn't expect you home for dinner. You've got to let us in on your plans if you want to eat with us." Krystal bends over to open the oven, revealing mammoth, sizzling steaks, the grease creating little pools of fire.

Chad moves behind Krystal to peer into the oven. "Yummy, Cupcake, yummy! Hmm, and so is this." He rubs her butt so that I have to look away.

Chad sloshes Scotch over ice cubes in two large tumblers. "Want one, Cupcake?"

"You know the answer to that, Chad," she replies flatly.

"Ah, Cupcake, I have to drink alone? Again?" He shrugs and looks at me. "What about you, boy? Let me buy you a drink."

If he's joking, it's not funny, and if he means it, it's sleazy. "No thanks. I'm in training." Being an athlete was a big part of who I am. It hurts to lie about it.

"You a running back?"

"He's a wrestler," says Monique, even though she knows I quit. Why are we pretending about this?

"All you high school boys know these days is pansy sports—wrestling, water polo, volleyball." Chad demonstrates each one, swinging his bowling-ball gut. "The only man's sport is football."

"Ha! Like you ever played," says Monique.

"I'm an armchair athlete, I'll admit, but I know quite a bit about it. Greatest sport there is." He raises his glass and toasts, "God bless football," then downs his drink with a rattle of ice cubes.

The hooker begins to hump my ankle. Wouldn't it be the pimp that would want to do that? I walk toward the living room as an excuse to nudge the dog off my foot. "Who plays?"

"What instrument?" asks Krystal. "I'm hecka good at pinball. Chad plays the piano."

"Just learning," he says.

"Play 'Mary Had a Little Lamb' for us," says Krystal.

"Play 'Hot Cross Buns,'" says Monique. "Ha! Chad can play a song about hot buns!" She and Krystal laugh together.

Chad strides across the living room. He sits at the piano, and Krystal and Monique hover around him. He weaves his fingers together, stretches out his arms, and cracks his knuckles all at once. He plays in a jerky motion, as the ladies nod in unison every time he presses a key. I don't know much about music, but I do know it's gotta have a beat.

When he finishes, he smiles proudly and the ladies clap.

"Isn't that good?" asks Monique. I think she's being sarcastic, but she looks sincere.

While Chad launches into "Hot Cross Buns," I inspect the pinball machine.

"Here, let me show you how this bad boy works," says Krystal.

Everybody knows how a pinball machine works, but I watch her play, hoping I'll get a turn. She's pretty good, but not that good. She cheers when she scores.

"Hey," says Chad, "*I'm* playing."

Monique begins to tinkle the highest keys on the piano. The dogs yap and leap backward as if the sound irritates them.

"Cut it out!" Chad leans toward the dogs and yells, "Shut up!"

Monique strikes the high keys again, and the pimp starts spinning in circles, then stops to lift his leg.

"Damn you, Monique!" shouts Krystal. "You always gotta cause trouble." She dashes to a spray bottle and rag set on the bar. She drops to her hands and knees and sprays and rubs the carpet where the dog has peed. Considering all the other brown spots on the white rug, it doesn't seem to do much good.

Monique begins to play pinball. When a ball rolls past a flipper, she rears the machine back on two legs.

"Get away!" Krystal screams at her, swatting at her with the pee rag.

Monique laughs and runs around the piano, dodging the rag and knocking Chad's music off the rack. Smoke billows out of the oven.

"Dinner's ready," Monique sings out.

Krystal runs to the kitchen, Chad yelling after her, "Ah, now, Cupcake, I thought you were watching the steaks. You know I like mine rare."

She opens the oven, and the smoke sets off the smoke alarm. The dogs yap and yap, their bulging eyes rolling back in their pinheads.

"Yum, yum," says Monique. "Charbroiled."

"Get out!" Krystal yells. "Kick 'em out, Big."

"We're going." Monique fumbles through a floppy, brown leather handbag set on the bar. She fishes out a wallet and extracts a card. She grabs her own bag, takes my hand, and pulls me out the front door.

"Aren't you glad you got to meet the fam?" she asks, her tone bitter with sarcasm. Her face is tense, and when I try to put my arm around her, she shrugs me off.

As we pass the *Mannekin Pis*, I say, "Now I get why they picked this fountain. It's warning people they're about to enter a house of dog piss."

My lame joke works its charm. She snuggles against my side and opens her hand, revealing the American Express card she jacked from her mom's purse. "Come on, baby. Let's eat."

Chapter Fifteen

The next morning, about eight o'clock, I say good-bye to my family, who thinks I'm headed over to school to catch the bus to Exeter for the second day of the wrestling invitational. Instead I drive over to Shelley's, where Monique has spent the night. I rap quietly on the backdoor, just like we planned, but no one answers. It's a little disappointing Monique isn't waiting on the other side of the door, eager to let me in, but I know how she loves to sleep. I knock a little harder, and finally Randi's three-year-old daughter, Jody, opens the door. The house is dark, with the blinds drawn, and cartoon sounds coming from the TV. I head down the hall to snuggle with my sleeping beauty on the futon, when I hear the scraping of a chair, the creak of a cupboard door, and the rustle of cereal raining down on the counter and floor. I return to the kitchen to find Jody covered in Frosty Flakes.

"I'm hungry," she says meekly, lifting a shoulder to protect her face, as if afraid of getting slapped.

"You're supposed to eat cereal, not wear it." I scoop as much cereal as I can back into the nearly empty box, pour some in a bowl with milk, and seat her at the table. While Jody eats, I finish the cleanup, wiping the counter and sweeping the floor.

The second time I start down the hallway, Jody calls after me, "Watch cartoons with me, Rafa."

"I want to see Monique."

"She's asleep and I'm lonely."

Monique might be cranky if I wake her up this early. "Okay. Maybe one cartoon."

It's weird sitting there on the couch with Jody, thinking about the wrestling meet going on, and me not being part of it. I talked to Diego last night, and he said the team was doing great, ahead in every weight category but one hundred fifty-two. I feel guilty I let my team down, but I know they can win without me.

When the cartoon is over, Jody begs me to stay for another. It's all good because Monique could sleep until noon; I still have plenty of time to snuggle with her. One cartoon blends into another until Monique staggers into the room, rubbing the sleep from her eyes, asking, "What are you doing here?"

It takes her a moment to completely wake up and remember we're spending the whole day together. The trouble with Goldhurst is that there's not much to do. There's the movies, but we went the day before. There's Starbucks, but how much coffee can you drink? Monique doesn't even like coffee; she drinks those fancy lattes. It's too cold in the park. It's too smelly and depressing sitting around with Shelley, Randi, and Randi's two little kids. At least we got a car.

We go to the IHOP for breakfast, and afterward Monique digs Krystal's American Express card out of her huge pink bag, which is set on her lap.

"Now what?" she asks.

"I don't know. The mall?"

"I'm tired of the mall. How about the flea market?"

Jesús opens his booth on Saturday mornings if he doesn't have a yard job to do. It would be pretty bad to come face-to-face with him when I'm supposed to be in Exeter at a meet. "They got nothing but junk," I say.

"It's something to do."

"None of those guys take American Express."

"Okay. Let's go to Pismo."

"Pismo Beach? Now? Are you out of your beautiful head?"

She shrugs slowly. "Why not? We got a car."

"Not if my mom ever found out, and she has her ways. It's a four-hour drive."

"Luke could do it in three and a half in that badass truck of his. Once we spent the whole night on the beach."

"We're going there so you can relive the memories?"

"You're cute when you're jealous." She wipes the dregs of her hot cocoa out of her mug and drops it into her bag.

"What are you doing?"

"I like the feel of that mug in my hand. Here." She reaches across the table, lifts my mug, and drops it into another section of her bag. "The next time we drink coffee together, we can be twinsies."

"You don't drink coffee."

"I know what we can do." She smiles a bit crookedly, a devilish glint in her eye.

When we get in the car, she directs me toward her house. I'm thinking maybe Krystal and Chad are gone with the yapping rats, and we can have the place to ourselves. I'm about to turn in to her subdivision, Golden Oak Ranch, when she says, "Not here. The next light."

We cross the canal and enter Royal Oak Ranch instead. Here the houses are all one-story, about half the size of Monique's house, and according to the billboard, a third of the cost. Only three model homes are completed and landscaped, but on each street other houses are in various stages of construction.

Monique directs me to park in front of the model home with a garage that's been converted into a sales office.

"What are we doing here?" I ask.

"Going shopping."

"For a house?"

She trails her hand up my thigh. "Come on. It will be an adventure."

She moves to get out of the car, but I pull her back by the hand. "This is crazy. They'll never believe us."

She rolls her nylon jacket into a smooth ball and arranges it under her sweater. "Yes, they will."

"Oh, no."

"Oh, yes. Come on, honey. I hope the nursery will have plenty of light."

Hand in hand, we walk up the driveway to the sales office. There are three selling agents, all of them pacing with no customers. It's early, and they've probably just opened. An elderly woman, whose name tag on her navy blazer reads Lois, peers at us over half glasses. "What can I do for you kids?"

I want to bolt, but Monique says, "We're looking to buy our first home."

Lois glances down at Monique's belly, then up again. "How lovely. What do you kids do for a living?"

"I'm substitute teaching for now, and he's just finishing up the police academy." The lies roll off Monique's tongue like they're rehearsed lines in a play. She shouldn't be doing hair and makeup for actors; she should *be* one.

I can tell what Lois is thinking: we don't have the dough. "Renting now, are you?"

"Oh, no. I live with my family, and he lives with his."

I nearly burst out laughing, I'm so shocked: Monique actually told the truth.

"My parents are buying the house for us," continues Monique. "You wouldn't expect them to put up with a crying baby, would you? They're kinda old and crabby."

Lois looks a bit more hopeful. "It is difficult for young married people to get a start in this economy without some help."

"Oh, we're not married. Who can afford a wedding? We'd rather wait a few years and have a house instead."

"First things first," says Lois.

She and another selling agent, Mike, give us a tour of the house, which is furnished so that it looks like people actually live there. There's a magazine open on the coffee table, a ceramic bowl of fruit on the counter, a table set for dinner with cloth napkins and candles, towels in the bathroom, and a few toys in the kid's room. The house is tiny. The kid's room only has space for one twin bed and a chest of drawers. A kid living in it wouldn't even have room for a few extra birthday presents. The yard is teeny too, just a ten-foot dirt strip between the house and fence. Rather than live in this brand-new house, I'd rather live in my old ghetto one; at least it's got some space to move around in.

Lois leads us through the house, pointing out all "the amenities," as she calls them. Meanwhile, Mike has popped ready-made cookie dough in the oven, and out come delicious-smelling chocolate chip cookies. We stand in the living room, chatting with Lois and munching cookies. Both Lois and Mike are treating us so seriously, I relax into my role of a soon-to-be-dad going through the police academy. Diego's big bro Ramón is a cop, so I know something about it.

Monique's hand moves to the side of her mouth, right where there's a smudge of chocolate. "Oh, Lois, do you mind if I take another quick peek at the bedroom? We've already bought the crib, and I'm not sure it will fit in that dinky little room. I'd like to stand back there and try to visualize it."

Lois's mouth tightens at the word *dinky*, but she waves her through. "Go ahead. Visualize away."

Monique is gone longer than I expected, and when she returns Lois and Mike lead us back to the sales office. Lois takes out a thick form from the desk and asks us to be seated.

Not even Monique can think of enough B.S. to fill that much paperwork, so she begs off. "Uh, we're really just looking this morning. We got a few more developments to see before we commit, but we're very interested, and we're almost sure to be back. It's such a darling little place, just like a dollhouse."

"Bring your folks next time," says Lois.

"We will. Oh!" Monique's hands fly to her padded stomach. "He's kicking me all the time lately." As we walk down the driveway, she lifts her hand over her head and waves.

I'm shaking with so much suppressed laughter, I can hardly walk. When we reach the car, I feel such a rush, I lift Monique off her feet and spin her around. I don't know if I'm happy because it was so much fun to fake those people out or because it's all over.

When we get into the car we laugh together, and I slap my knee. "You were great. You really had them going. That was wild."

"Oh, we're not done having fun yet." Monique grins like a crazed person.

Late that afternoon we're driving around, and Monique says, "Drop me off at home. I've got some stuff to do for a couple hours."

I'm disappointed because when we planned to spend the day together, I thought it would be the whole day, every minute of it. "What stuff?"

She doesn't reply at first. Her face is clouded over, secretive, and immediately I get jealous, thinking Luke is lurking just around the corner in his truck. Finally she says, "Bra shopping."

"Bra shopping?"

"Uh-huh. With my mom."

"With your mom? I didn't know you did stuff like that with your mom."

"We hella bond over bra shopping."

"She better not reach for her American Express card."

"Why not? It will be there. I slip it in and out of her wallet all the time."

"Doesn't she notice the extra charges on her bill?"

"No. Why would she?"

I just shake my head. It's a strange world Monique lives in, like her family and mine live on different planets.

By then we're in front of her house. "Pick me up around seven," she says. "We'll have another adventure."

We've been racking our brains the whole day trying to think up stuff to do. "Another adventure?"

"Stop repeating me. You sound like a tard." She kisses me and bounds out of the car.

Now what do I do? Half of me wants to lurk around the corner, waiting to see if Luke shows up. The other half says that's totally messed up. I can't be seen by my family members or any friends of my mom who might tell her they saw me. It totally sucks not to be where I'm supposed to be. I end up hanging out at the public library, sitting at one of those little study stalls and napping on my folded arms like a homeless bum.

Chapter Sixteen

When I pick up Monique later that evening, she's carrying her backpack like we're going on a study date, as if she knows what the word *study* means. Under her pink parka she's got on a purple silky dress, stockings, and high heels. Of course I've got on what I've been wearing all day—jeans, flannel shirt, and hoodie.

When she steps into the car, I exclaim, "Whoa, baby. You look hot. What's the occasion?"

"Our adventure."

"Oh, right. What color is it?"

"What?"

"You know. Your new bra."

"Oh, that! That didn't work out. Drive over this way."

Of course I'm wondering what she *did* do.

She nods across the canal, toward Royal Oak Ranch. "We're going back."

"They're not open."

"We don't want them to be."

"You crazy, baby? That's breaking and entering."

She smiles angelically. "Just entering. Remember when I went back to have another look at the bedroom? I unlocked a window."

"You're bad," I say, a mix of fear and exhilaration rising in my chest.

We park at the side of the road, at the edge of an orchard. The white barricade before us prevents cars from crashing into the canal that runs between the two subdivisions.

"We'll have to wait here until the coast is clear." Monique pulls a blanket out of her backpack and arranges it across our laps. It's cozy in the car, romantic even, with the moonlight streaming down on us. Occasionally we see the security guard drive slowly through the streets of unfinished houses.

"There he goes," she says, pointing to the departing car. "On his coffee break. He won't be back for a while. Going to meet his girlfriend at Starbucks."

"How do you know so much?"

"The dude guards our subdivision, too. I was walking the dogs one morning, and he yelled at me from his car. I thought he might be a perv, but he just asked me for some ointment for burns. He'd scalded his lap with spilled coffee, and he couldn't call in for help because he's not allowed to leave on a break. We got to talking, about his girlfriend and all that."

We're still laughing as we get out of the car. We cross the footbridge and head for the model home we toured earlier. The whole time I'm thinking—hoping—we're not really going in. Probably Lois or Mike checked the window and locked it. We walk behind the house and cross the strip of dirt they call a backyard.

Sure enough, the window slides open smoothly. "Ta-da! Open, says me!" Monique holds out her hand like a queen, and I grasp it while she climbs through the window. I follow her. Of course we can't turn on any lights, but with the moonlight and the streetlights, we can see well enough. It's creepy though, like we're burglarizing a real residence, the inhabitants asleep in their beds. I actually hesitate at the window, expecting to hear breathing.

Monique heads straight for the dining area. She takes two of the four place settings off the table and dusts the two remaining plates and wineglasses with one of the cloth napkins. From her backpack, she removes cheese, salami, French bread, a thick bar of chocolate, and finally, a bottle of red wine.

"I stole it from Chad's wine cellar. I sure as hell hope it's not a two-hundred-dollar bottle that he'll miss."

"He pays that much for one bottle of wine?"

"Yep. And to me, a seven-dollar bottle tastes about the same. He's just out to impress people, mainly my mom, and she doesn't even drink."

"I noticed."

"It pisses her off that he tries to get her to. He thinks she can drink moderately, but she knows she can't." Monique leans over the table, her dark eyes round. "She can never forgive herself for the accident. Shelley almost lost a leg." She extracts a corkscrew and a bread knife. Clearly she's thought of everything. It's not like her to plan something. Usually she's all spur of the moment. This feels really special, that she spent her afternoon planning this. We clink glasses and take sips of wine. It goes down smooth.

"I don't think she likes me," I say. "Shelley, I mean. She's always giving me the evil eye."

"That's her good one. The other one's glass."

"Oh! My bad."

"It's okay. Most people don't know. She's really smart, you know. Supergood in math. She's going to be a CPA, and they make bank."

"What's that stand for?"

"Don't you know nothing? It's somebody who takes care of rich people's money, and then they get rich themselves."

"How does that work?"

"Hell if I know."

We dig into our secret, moonlit feast. With no one living in the development, it's real quiet.

We talk on and on, saying more to each other than we ever have before. I tell her about my dad leaving us when Jojo was a baby, and how Jesús has been living with us for about eight years. She tells me that after the accident her parents went to Alcoholics Anonymous and started attending church. "This went on about three years, until Pastor Ted caught Dad having sex with Ashley, who was the youth ministry director, right on the floor of the youth ministry activities room. Pastor shipped her out to an affiliated church in Texas, then counseled my parents, trying to save their marriage. It didn't work, of course. Dad followed Ashley down to Texas the first chance he could get."

"My mom would call her a home wrecker."

"I don't think it was her fault. My dad wanted her and went after her, and she was no match for him. She was inexperienced, fresh out of a Christian university, probably a virgin. When Chad and Mom first got married, I couldn't stand living with them, so I begged to go live with my dad. I lasted one semester. I'd sit back and watch them interact as a family— prayers before dinner, prayers at bedtimes, prayers over the paddle before their two little girls got a swat—but they're really happy, you know? Dad would get down on the floor and play dolls with the girls, and I'd think Leah could be Shelley, Rachel could be me. He made a mess of his first family, so now he has a second chance with this one. I didn't fit in. I decided to get myself kicked out. I got caught naked with a guy in the master bedroom jacuzzi."

"That's not so bad," I say hopefully, because she didn't

mention what she and the guy were actually *doing*. "What did they do about it?"

"When I looked Ashley in the eye, I saw fear. She was really afraid of the damage I could do to her precious little family, but I also saw forgiveness. I saw that no matter what I did, she would never kick me out—because I'm her husband's daughter, just like her own two little girls. I would have to be so terrible, I wouldn't even be able to stand myself. So I just went home on my own. Shelley can never forgive our dad for leaving and hasn't spoken to him since. Know why she watches those *telenovelas* on TV?"

I shrug. "I thought she was studying Spanish."

"Ha! That really hot guy with a mustache and gold jewelry who runs around with no shirt on, grabbing and shaking women—well, he looks sorta like our dad. When he left us I was really too young to understand. All I learned from it is men come and go."

"You don't believe in forever?"

"Not when it comes to guys."

"I could prove you wrong," I say hopefully. Wiping crumbs off the front of me, I swipe my bulging hoodie pouch. "Oh, I forgot! I have something for you."

"For me? A present? What is it?"

"Close your eyes."

I go around to her side of the table, set the rainbow-colored knit cap on her head, and tie the strings beneath her chin.

She gently pats the wool. "Oh, it's soft. Let me see." She slides the cap off her head. "Oh, how sweet! Would you believe it? I almost bought one just like it."

"I know. I saw you."

"At the flea market? I didn't see you. Why didn't you say hi?"

127

I shrug. "You were with Luke. You were arguing and—"

"Hey! That was *before* we got together."

I don't dare tell her I was actually trying to *sell* those caps. I just nod shyly. "I've liked you a long time."

"Aw, it's perfect. I love cute little Mexican things." She tugs the hat back on.

"Salvadoran."

"Huh?"

"It's handmade in El Salvador."

"Whatever!" She takes out a little mirror and spends some time arranging certain parts of her hair to flow out of the cap. Satisfied with the way it looks, she begins to cut the bar of chocolate. "Hey, you know the two things that go together better than anything? Red wine and dark chocolate." She places a chunk of chocolate on her tongue and passes it into my mouth. She holds her glass to my lips. "Now sip. Good?"

"Mmm."

"Wouldn't it be great if we could really live together, and be alone whenever we wanted to, in our own little cozy house?"

"Yeah," I say, dreaming into the future.

"Me and Luke were planning to get an apartment, soon as he graduates in June."

"You'd still be in high school!"

"So? My mom would've let me, but his mom said we couldn't. She said she wanted him to live at home while he gets his auto technology certificate. I think really it's cuz she never liked me."

I shake my head. "I thought you wanted to do hair and makeup for the stars."

"Everyone has dreams like that, but you know they never come true."

I know what she's talking about. I was going to win the state championship and get a scholarship, and now I'm not even in wrestling.

"Hey, maybe we could get an apartment after we get out of high school. Chad and Mom would be so happy to get rid of me, they'd set us up, just like they do for Shelley."

"My mom is the opposite. She's raising me to be independent."

"That's so old-fashioned. How can you stand it? Maybe that's what makes you a geek. For reals, Rafa, you came off as a tard until I started going out with you."

I know how I must look to my classmates, running off to the flea market on Fridays, doing yard work most Saturdays, driving a dumpy car and eating lunch out of a brown bag. Somehow all of that seems better than the way Monique's family does things.

When we move into the bedroom, it's disappointing to pull back the bedspread and find a bare mattress. It makes me realize we're just playing house. I never entirely relax. I keep thinking about getting caught. That would be one of the worst—getting arrested buck naked.

Close to midnight, we start cleaning everything up. Monique washes the dishes and replaces the four place settings just as we found them. She collects all our garbage in a plastic bag and stuffs it in her backpack.

After giving everything a final inspection, she asks, "Have we forgotten anything?"

"I don't think so. They'll never know we were here."

"We should check the bedroom." She tilts the ceramic fruit bowl in her hands. "Krystal's birthday is coming up. This would be the perfect thing."

"You could buy her one just like it."

"With what? Her own American Express card? That wouldn't be right." She dumps the fruit out on the counter. "I'm taking this one."

I look at the fruit scattered on the counter. "Isn't that a little too obvious?"

"Okay." She stuffs all the fruit in her backpack, mashing it down so it will all fit. She slings the backpack over her shoulders and holds the huge bowl in front of her.

"You're going to walk down the street carrying stolen property? What if the security guard catches you?"

"That idiot? He wouldn't notice if his nose was missing."

"Monique . . ."

"Okay!" She slips the bowl under her pink parka. "Looks like we're back to having a baby, baby." She smiles so sweetly I have to laugh.

We creep out the window and lurk around the house, waiting for the security guard to slowly drive by. Then we make a run for it across the footbridge. We tumble into the car, hugging and laughing.

Her wide grin fades as she pats her head. "Oh, no. I did leave something behind. My little cap. I left it on the nightstand."

"Are you sure? I didn't see it there."

"It must've slipped off. We gotta go back for it."

"No! Never return to the scene of a crime."

She slaps my forearm—hard. "You *made* me leave it. You gave me so much grief about this god damn *bowl*"—she hurls it out the car window like a pregnant Frisbee—"that I forgot my own darling cap!"

"Calm down, I'll—"

"Don't *ever* tell me to calm down." She begins tossing fruit after the shattered bowl, one spoiled piece at a time.

"I'll get you another cap. The guy who sells them has a whole truckload of them."

"It wouldn't be the one you picked out for me, and carried around, and waited for just the right moment to give to me. It wouldn't be my own darling cap."

I'm shocked and flustered by her outburst. I never figured she'd be sentimental. She pummels my thigh with her fists, until I place my hands over hers to still them.

Chapter Seventeen

One morning when I get to school, the car parked in front of me is decorated with balloons, Silly String, and paper flowers. Across the rear window, printed in pink lipstick, is

> RYAN
>
> YOU, ME, SADIE'S?
>
> LUV U, MEGAN

In American lit, Mr. Espinoza turns on the overhead and all the kids laugh. The screen says

> MATT FRANKLIN
>
> WILL YOU GO TO SADIE'S WITH ME?
>
> DANIELLE

At lunch, Monique and me eat at a table on the quad. I'm having my usual brown-bag special, but I bought her chicken strips, fries, and a soda with the last few bucks I had.

Some kids begin to gather around the table next to us, all of them dressed in black, so I know it's Tor's group. I'm able to peer between two guys to see a girl dipping a fry in catsup and using it as a brush to paint a Sadie's invitation on the tabletop. It looks like blood, and the kids laugh and shriek. I gaze out across the quad and smile.

Monique kicks my sole. "What?"

"Oh, nothin'," I say, feeling my grin stretch.

"Tell me."

"Okay. I'm just wondering how you're gonna ask me to Sadie's."

"Oh, that. We gotta talk about that." She's concentrating on swirling a fry through catsup, as if that's the most important thing she has to do. I think she's going to tell me she doesn't want to go or her parents won't give her the money, and that's okay with me. "Don't kill me, Rafa. I already asked Luke."

"What?" The school yard begins to spin.

"I invited him a long time ago."

"Doesn't he assume it's off? Isn't that what breaking up means? All future plans canceled?"

"It's not that easy. We're still friends, and he already—"

"Bought his dress?"

"You don't have to be nasty about it." She scoops a pool of catsup onto her tongue with the fry she's been twirling.

I'm so angry I can't stand the sight of her. As I swing my legs over the bench, my toe catches, and I'm reeling face-first toward the cement. A firm hand in a long black lace glove with cutout fingers grips my forearm, preventing a humiliating fall. I peer up the lacy arm into Tor's face. I can tell by her knowing look that she overheard our argument.

"Easy there, cowboy," she says.

I free my toe and sprint through campus and across the field to the rear parking lot. I want to jump into my car and drive away, but the bell will soon ring, and I can't be truant. I cross the street and enter the park. I pass the jungle gym and a cluster of tables, where a guy and girl are talking, their foreheads pressed together, their arms on each other's shoulders.

I run until I can't run any farther, then stand on the bank of the creek, staring into the rushing water. I've been wondering where Luke Jefferson has been all this time. So now he's just a friend—like hell! Where was she those hours last Saturday, when she just had to be apart from me? If he's still doing her, I'll kill him.

I pick up a rock and throw it. I hurl stone after stone into the water. The splashes soak my feet, but I don't care. I wonder how I fell for such a heartless, two-faced bitch. If I could stop loving her this second, I'd be better off. I can't. Already I want to go crawling back to her and make up.

"Rafa! Hey, Rafa!" It's a girl's voice, but not Monique's.

I turn around and see Andy coming up to me. She's always coming up to me. Any time now she's going to ask me to Sadie's, and I'm going to have to break her heart.

She places her hands on her hips. "What's this bullshit about quitting wrestling?"

"It's a waste of time."

"It's your sport! You love it."

"I'm sick of it. I'm sick of everything."

"What about college?"

"What about it? I'll never make it through. I'm not going to amount to shit."

"You take that back."

"It's true. I'm the biggest loser you'll ever know."

"Take it back!" She grabs me by the shoulders and starts to sort of wrestle with me. It's a stupid, awkward move, and she knows better. It seems like she's fooling around, but her face tells me she's not. She shoots, going for my hamstrings.

"Hey, cut it out." I need to fling my legs back into a sprawl, but I don't have the energy or the will. Too late I try to wriggle out of her hold, but she's strong and determined, and I don't care what happens to me. She takes me down and pins me.

"Hey, ow!" There's a good reason for those mats.

She presses me against the cold, hard ground. This is the time in a match when the victor jumps up and lends a hand to his opponent, especially if he's a teammate, but she sits on my heaving, aching chest and won't let me up.

I look up at Andrea, breathing heavily through parted lips, her blue eyes jumping with rage, tiny beads of sweat forming at her blond hairline.

I see it then, as if slowly waking from a dream and not knowing what's real and what's not: she's beautiful. I imagine her in my arms at Sadie's, Monique glaring at us, her eyes narrowed in jealousy. I'd be tempted to go with Andy, if I wasn't so sick of being taken down by girls.

I lie still, not even trying to get out from under her. "There. Happy? Why don't you try acting like a girl for a change?"

"I do what I want. That's the way it's supposed to work."

"Supposed to, but it doesn't. Everyone's always judging you."

"Who the hell cares?"

"Everyone. Like maybe if you weren't always competing against guys, one might like you." Her face goes slack, but I don't let up. It feels good to slam someone, instead of me being the one who gets dumped on all the time. "Act like a girl, and maybe if you asked a guy to Sadie's, he might go with you."

She slides off me and sits on her folded legs beside me, her hands resting on her thighs, her lower lip slightly jutted forward. "What are you talking about, Rafa? I asked Diego, and of course he's going with me."

"You did?"

"Well, yeah. We're going out. Haven't you noticed?"

"Guess not." Diego walks slowly up to us, a bit shyly. I realize then, they were the couple hanging out at the park table, and Andy spotted me and decided it was an opportunity to confront me about quitting wrestling. It's pretty awkward, with Diego standing there, having just watched me roll around with his girlfriend. I scramble to my feet and brush the grass and dirt from my clothes.

"How's it going?" he says.

"Okay." I nod at him like I've got no troubles at all.

"I miss ya, man. We should hang out."

"For sure." I know we won't. I know he doesn't approve of Monique, and he knows that's why I've been avoiding him.

Diego takes Andy's hand and pulls her up, their arms sliding around each other's waists in one smooth motion. They fit together perfectly. Popular Diego and tomboy Andy—I never dreamed they'd get together, and yet it seems so right. If I was any kind of friend to either one of them, I would have seen it coming. These days, I don't have the energy to pay attention to anybody but Monique.

They amble slowly away, their heads pressed together.

"Hey," Diego says, down low. "I saw you take down Rafa. It was hot."

"Shut up," she says, and slaps his butt.

That afternoon while I'm driving home, America spots a McDonald's and asks me to stop, but not really expecting me to. Mom wouldn't approve of us spoiling our dinner and wasting money on junk food, but I could use a treat. Usually I'm in a hurry to dump Jojo and America home so I can get with Monique, but not today. Since lunch, she's texted me seventeen times, or at least that's the number of times my phone vibrated in my pocket through Algebra Two and chemistry. The problem is I have to admit to America that I'm broke.

Jojo pulls a wad of crumpled bills out of his monster jeans and says, "We're good."

I don't even want to know where he got all that cash; I just let him buy for us. It's kinda fun, the three of us hanging out, something we hardly ever do. It's sunny for late October, and we sit outside so that America can play on the playground after she finishes her sundae. Jojo doesn't have anything to say as he shovels in his super-sized fries, and I'm busy with my own thoughts as I chomp down on a Big Mac. Jojo used to depend on me a lot more when we were younger, and he looked up to me, but now that he's in middle school we hardly ever talk anymore. I have no clue what he's up to, but I can bet it's no good. Still, it's consoling to be sitting here with him, watching America jump into a vat of balls, while I stuff my face.

"Hey, dawg, isn't that like off-limits?" asks Jojo.

"What?"

"That big ole burger. I never seen you eat something like that before."

I shake my head. "Quit wrestling."

"For reals?" He narrows his eyes, like he doesn't believe me. "Isn't that like your whole main thing?"

"Just ain't feeling it no more."

"I hear you. Least you can eat anything you want now."

I nod, my mouth too full to reply.

"And you won't have to ever worry about getting matched up with no girl again. That'd be the worst, I think. When you win, it's like you beat a *girl*. When you lose, you like lose to a *girl*. Whoa. It's like a lose-lose situation. Know what I mean?"

"Sure do, dawg." I quit wrestling, but girls are still taking me down. I want to change the subject, but can only think of Mom-type questions. "How's school going?"

"Piece of cake."

I laugh. "Wasn't that way when I went to middle school."

"It is now. Like they changed it to just benchmarks. We don't even get letter grades. Just ones, twos, threes, and fours."

"Huh?"

"Yeah, man. Like if you forget your binder or pencil, they can't grade you down. Miss an assignment—that's cool, too. You just gotta take these little benchmarks, and you can take them over and over till you pass. It's all on the teachers, dawg. If their students don't pass, they get like low pay or arrested or something."

We slap our knees, thinking about a teacher getting hauled off in handcuffs. It feels good to laugh.

What I forget is that report cards are due. Usually either me or Jojo snatches them out of the mailbox before Mom gets to them, especially the first one of the school year. But when we get home, there they are: three report cards laid out on the kitchen table. Jojo's right. He's got no worries, all 3s and 4s, the best report card he's ever had, and of course America has straight As. Only mine sucks. Ds and Fs, except for an A in weight training.

After receiving her hugs and pats on the head, America dashes off to watch cartoons in the living room, while me and Jojo hang out in the kitchen with Mom and Jesús. I wonder why Jojo doesn't leave too, but I guess he wants to stick around and gloat over me catching hell for a change, instead of him.

"A D in Spanish, *mijo*. How could you?" asks Mom.

"It's Spanish Three! It's got tons of rules, like when to use the imperfect or the preterite."

Mom crinkles her nose like she doesn't know what I'm talking about. Her Spanish is fluent, of course, but I hear her making some of the grammar mistakes Señora Luna points out in class. Jesús' Spanish, on the other hand, is precise and formal, with a much larger vocabulary.

"How are you going to get into college with these grades?" Mom asks.

I hold my palms up. "Hey, it's just the quarter, only a progress report. I'll bring them up by the end of semester."

She shakes the miserable paper in my face. "This means academic probation! You're off the wrestling team!"

"I quit wrestling," I say flatly.

"What? When?"

I shrug. "Don't know. Like a couple of weeks ago."

"Oh? And when were you going to get around to telling us?"

"It doesn't even matter. I can't wrestle anyway."

"It does matter! And so do all your deceptions." Mom springs up from her chair to bend over me, hands on her hips. "It's that girl, isn't it, *mijo*?"

"No! I just needed a break."

"Mother of God, she's ruining your life!"

"*Tranquila, Bonita, tranquila.*" Jesús takes Mom's hands in both of his and leads her back to her chair. As she cries, he offers her one Kleenex after another, strokes her hair, and coos in Spanish.

The greasy Big Mac does somersaults in my gut. There's

no worse feeling for a Mexican boy than to make his mother cry. I think I have no right to my life. My mom never should have suffered the pains of childbirth to bring me into this world.

Finally, she blows her nose and dries her eyes.

Jesús looks at me with his long face and says, "*Mijo, de joven yo era como tú.*" When I was a teenager, I was much like you.

I don't believe him, of course. How could this old Salvadoran guy be anything like me?

Chapter Eighteen

Jesús begins his story, speaking quietly in Spanish. He speaks slowly and directly at me, so I understand most of it. When I don't, I look at Mom, and she translates or explains. Jojo and I sit there and listen, not because we're interested, but out of respect. It's not long before we're leaning forward, straining our ears and Spanish skills to catch every word.

"In my country, children are required to attend school only until the age of thirteen, and many—over half—of the children in my little town did not attend at all. Nobody cared. My parents were poor, but they came from good families who valued education. They did not trust the public schools of the military government, but sent us to the priests and nuns. All of my seven brothers and sisters graduated from high school, all but me. To me, school was boring. Why should I sit on a hard wooden bench all day, listening to the old priest drone on about the rules of Latin, when I could be like the other boys, running off on my own adventures?

"By age twelve I was restless and reckless. I would hike high into the mountains, eating wild papayas and drinking from streams, dropping to the ground to sleep away the night, and then hike some more the next day. Or I would stay out all night drinking with my friends. When I returned home, my mother would read from the Scriptures about the Prodigal Son. My father would ask her why she wasted her breath on an idler like me, when she had so many dutiful, productive children. At school, Father Rafael would lecture me, calling me an intelligent boy who sinned by squandering his God-given talents. He laid out pink stripes on my palms with his ruler. Worst of all, I was to spend the day copying pages and pages of my Latin grammar book. None of this stopped me from running away again.

"This was a time of civil war in El Salvador. The oppressive government took away our freedom and gave us nothing in return. Only the Catholic Church was willing to help us. The priests and nuns gathered together our small, poor farms and created bigger, more efficient ones. The corn and beans we grew kept us from starving, but the government viewed our agricultural cooperatives as communism and began a crackdown. Many priests and nuns were tortured, killed, and mutilated. Our bishop was assassinated while saying mass. People disappeared from their homes and were never heard from again or were found slain in the fields. Our people fought back. They formed guerrilla units to combat the National Guard. Many people died, more than eighty thousand.

"Everybody was afraid. My older brother Juan was at the university in San Salvador, but when one of his professors and many students were killed, he had to go into hiding. We didn't know where he was, alive or dead. He was the best of all of us, my parents' great hope for a more prosperous life. My father began to walk slower and slower, his eyes to the ground. My mother went to bed one night and could not get up for many weeks.

"While all of this was going on, I sat on my hard bench copying my Latin grammar book. What good did it do when my countrymen all around me were dying, crushed under the boot of oppression, losing their fight for justice? I felt stupid and useless.

"One night the National Guard of El Salvador came for Father Rafael. They cut off his hands and hanged him by his feet from the church bell rope. The next day when the wind blew, his lifeless body tolled the bell, low and moaning. When I got to school, I knelt before him and wept. I asked myself why I would love a man who beat my hands, but I knew he was the only person in all the world who expected great things from me. I promised him I would do something to help my people. But what could I do, a boy of only fifteen? I had no stomach for killing, not even the cruel soldiers who murdered unarmed civilians.

"I did find a way to help. With my knowledge of the mountains, I could show the guerrilla units good places to make their hidden camps. I carried messages, provisions, and weapons from unit to unit. I was gone from home many months. When I returned, my mother told me the National Guard had knocked on our door looking for me. They searched all the rooms and questioned my family. I knew if I remained at home I would put my family in danger. My parents asked many relatives to take me in, but all of them were afraid. I journeyed to San Salvador in search of my brother Juan and found him living in the house of his slain professor's widow. She passed him off as a nephew, but the appearance of a second "nephew" would cause suspicion among her neighbors. I had no choice but to seek sanctuary in a Catholic church.

"This church was communicating with Catholic churches in cities throughout the United States, which were willing to grant sanctuary to Salvadorans. I did not want to leave my country, but also I did not want to die. A nun gave me papers to carry. They were in English, and I did not know what they said. The sister told me they were instructions about reporting to the courts in San Francisco, where I would be granted a legal guest visa for political asylum until the civil war ended and I could return home safely.

"The day I was to board the bus out of San Salvador, the terminal was crowded with many other refugees attempting to flee the country. National Guardsmen roamed the premises searching for enemies of the state. They searched each bus and pulled off people seemingly at random—young men and old, a group of nuns, one entire family. When a guardsman entered my bus, I thought, My life is over, this is the day I die. I took out my rosary and bowed my head to pray for my soul. I did not look up again until I felt the bus rumbling out of the terminal.

"Many bus rides later, I came to live in the dark basement of a Catholic church in San Francisco. At first there were only twenty-three of my countrymen there, then sixty, then more. The Church tried to find jobs for us as dishwashers, maids, gardeners, baby-sitters, and they would cash for us the checks we were given. I wanted one of those jobs, but many people were in line ahead of me, and those who spoke English were employed first. You think I don't know English now, well I knew nothing then. I sat in that smelly, crowded church basement, wishing for my Latin grammar book and the hard bench of my old school. I wished I had never run away or tried to help the guerrillas. Heroes fight until their deaths. Only cowards run away and hide in another country. I was only sixteen, but felt at the end of my life.

"I begged for work to do. I did not care even if I was paid for it. A priest put me on a truck going around to houses of the parishioners to collect their rummage—old clothes and blankets—for the refugees. All these things were collected in a few weeks, and then I was back, spending my days in the basement, dreaming of the mountains of my country and the faces of the people I had left behind.

"One day a contractor came looking for men to pick strawberries in Santa Maria. He said the men didn't need to know English, nor did they need to have legal documents to work for him. The farmers paid him for all the pickers, and then he paid the workers. I had never heard of such an arrangement, and I didn't know where Santa Maria was, but I liked its name, St. Mary, the mother of God. I was eager to be out in the fresh air, working in the fields. I knew if I joined the picking crew, I would miss the court date on my legal papers, but I went with the contractor anyway.

"I did not know the work would be so hard, and the handle on my hoe so short it could break my back. The contractor paid us little of the money we earned, but since we were given so much less in El Salvador, it seemed adequate. Half of the first pay I earned, I sent to my parents, and it was enough for my whole family to eat for a month.

"After strawberry season, cotton was ripe in Corcoran, and after that, grapes were ready to be picked and dried for raisins in Fresno, and then in Sanger the nectarine orchards needed to be pruned, and after that near Goldhurst, the orange harvest began. Soon the strawberries in Santa Maria were ripe once again.

"The days were long, but the years were short. The civil war in El Salvador ended, but there was no work for me in my country. My parents were getting old, my brother and sisters needed to stay in school. My family needed me to work in the United States and send money home to them. Eventually, I saved enough to buy my van.

"One night in October, I was drinking beer in a pizza parlor in Goldhurst with some men, all Mexican. We were not friends, but our hunger and thirst caused us to pass an evening together. We raised our mugs, and one of the men said, 'What do we drink to?'

"'It is my birthday,' I told them, suddenly remembering.

"'How old are you?' one of them asked me.

"I had not thought about the answer to that question in many years. I had to stop and count up on my fingers all the years that I had been living in the United States. I could not believe it. The sixteen-year-old boy who had dropped out of school to save his country was now a twenty-eight-year-old exile who had no prospects of returning home ever again.

"I drank a lot of beer that night. I made my last mug salty with my tears."

Jesús has talked for a long time, speaking enough words to last him a year. Jojo's mouth is agape; Mom is smiling. Jesús takes a drink of water and taps my report card. "Don't make the same mistake I did, *mijo*. Take advantage of your education. You will do better next time, *verdad*?" Jesús places his palms on the table to slowly ease his aching back out of the chair.

"That's it?" exclaims Jojo. "That's the end of the story?"

Jesús shrugs. "*Sí.*"

"Oh, no. I wanna know how you got—" Jojo raises one arm over his head and crashes four spread fingers onto the kitchen table. We all laugh, not just because it's a funny gesture, but because Jojo likes to act like he doesn't care about any of us.

Jesús continues in Spanish. "Not long after I spent the evening crying in my beer, I had the luckiest day of my life. I met your mamá, my *Bonita*."

"Where?" asks Jojo. "A bar?"

Mom slaps his arm playfully. "The laundromat! A neighbor was taking care of you boys. You were so little then, three and seven, and such a handful! I had a dozen errands to run that morning, so I left our clothes in the dryer as I dashed around like crazy. When I returned to the laundromat the dryer I was using was still going, but it was drying someone else's clothes. I looked around for our pile of clothes but didn't see them. I looked at all the clothes the other women in the laundromat were folding and packing in their baskets, suspicious that they might be stealing our things right under my nose! I didn't find them. My heart began to race because nearly all our clothes decent enough to wear were now missing, and I had little money to replace them. Finally, I noticed this guy folding Jojo's overalls, going over and over them, like he was ironing them with his hands. Nearly all our wash was folded, separated into neat stacks. I went up to him to see what was going on."

Jesús adds in Spanish, "At first I was embarrassed to be caught folding someone else's clothes. I explained to your mamá that I needed a dryer, and all of them had been taken. The one Mamá had been using had been idle for twenty minutes. I thought if I folded the clothes that I removed from the dryer, then the owner would not mind so much."

"Say what?" asks Jojo.

Mom translates, then adds, "Jesús' accent was one of the first things I noticed about him. 'You are not Mexican,' I said to him, and he began to tell me his life story, much like he just told you now. I thought I was in a big hurry, but for once I had met an interesting man, one who also seemed kind and considerate, and so I took the time to talk to him. We talked for so long, Jesús' drying finished. I insisted on helping him fold his laundry."

"Again I was embarrassed," says Jesús, "because my clothes were so ragged, especially *mi ropa interior*."

Mom laughs. "They were the holiest underwear I had ever seen, but I said, 'You know, these will be like new if I put a few stitches in them. Come home with me and meet my boys. Have some lunch with us, and I'll fix them right up.'"

"It was great to meet you guys," says Jesús. "Jojo, you were a happy, busy little guy, and, Rafael, when I learned you had the same name as my beloved, assassinated Latin teacher, I knew it was a sign from God. Your mamá never mended my underwear, though."

Mom covers his hand with hers and smiles at him. "I did not want to hurt your feelings, but they were beyond repairing. It was so much easier to pick up another couple of packages at Kmart." She turns to us. "But he fixed plenty of things for us: the leaky faucets, the caulking around the tub, the loose boards in the fence, the ripped screen door. I could get used to this, I thought. It had been a long time since there was a man around the house."

"So that is why you kept me," says Jesús, laughing with his eyes. "You needed a handyman."

Mom pats his hand. "That's not all I needed. I liked the naps I got to take when you took the boys to play in the park. And breakfast in bed with your thick Salvadoran tortillas and rich, black coffee. I could get used to this, I thought. And I did. When it came time to harvest the strawberries that year, I talked Jesús into staying with us."

"And I forgot about ever returning to El Salvador. When I became your papá, *muchachos*, you, *mi familia*, became my country. You are the whole world to me. Soon after that, Mamá and I decided to have a child together, and in time, America was born."

"If you loved your country so much, why did you name America after ours?" I ask. "You could have named her Salvadora, or just plain Dora."

"El Salvador is in America—Central America," says Jesús. "There are many countries in America, and we are all Americans."

That night, I have a hard time going to sleep, my mind filled with murder, mutilations, and mayhem. I wonder what it would be like to live in a country where soldiers pulled citizens out of bed and shot them before their families. I figure Jojo has been asleep a long time, when his voice breaks the dark silence.

"Hey, dawg, you awake?"

"Yeah."

"You believe that wild story Jesús was telling us?"

"Jesús, a hero, out to save his country?"

"Didn't sound right to me neither." It's quiet again, except for the soft slurping sounds his thumb-sucking makes. He adds, "But who could make up a story like that?"

"Well, maybe it's partly true. Maybe he just exaggerated."

"Yeah, dawg. You got it."

There's no use pretending, though. Our opinion of Jesús has changed forever.

Chapter Nineteen

Next Saturday, Sadie's night, I'm hanging out with America, listening to her read a Goosebumps book. She's curled up on the sofa, her legs tucked under her, her hair wafting the Fandango Tangerine shampoo she's always raving about. The weight of her head resting against my upper arm is somehow consoling. Her high, expressive voice washes over me, while inside my own thoughts churn. Now he's picking her up. Now they're eating dinner. Now they're driving to the dance, getting their picture taken together, holding each other in a slow dance.

"What's wrong, Rafa?"

"Nothin'. Why?"

"You just kinda went stiff."

"I did? Just flexing."

Since Tuesday, me and Monique have sort of patched things up. A couple of times she's tried to explain why she couldn't cancel out on Luke: it's rude, it's a dis, it would hurt him, she doesn't want to cause any drama. I'm not buying any of it, especially the last one. Monique is all about drama. She wants to get all glammed up for him, but why? To show him what he's been missing, or to try to get him back? It's driving me crazy.

My phone vibrates in my pocket, and I check the caller ID. It's Tor, which surprises me. She hardly ever calls me, and I know Moldy Muffin is playing at Sadie's, which means this is not a good time for her to chat.

When I answer, she says, "I got bad news and good news," her tone singing with amusement. "The bad news is that Luke is here with another girl."

"What's the good news?"

"The good news is that Luke is here with another girl." Her peals of laughter are thick with derision.

"How is that good news?"

"Ha! Don't you think *she* deserves it?"

"Yeah," I admit bitterly. "So who's the girl?"

"Dunno. Lemme me text around, see what I can find out. We're going on in a few minutes, though."

"Okay." I'm about to hang up when I think of something I often forget when it comes to Tor. "Uh, Tor? Thanks."

"Roger, buddy. Over and out."

I snap my phone shut.

"You should turn off your phone when someone is reading to you," says America. "It's only common courtesy."

"Common courtesy? You should hear yourself sometime, my country. You talk like a grown-up."

As America continues to read, my thoughts are flying. Luke didn't cancel out on Monique; she would have told me. It's unlikely he found a date at the last minute, which means he must have been planning this for some time. She's going to take it hard, but what can I do about it?

"Are you paying attention to the story?" America asks me. "It doesn't seem like it."

"I'm getting it. The dummy came alive."

"Duh."

My phone sounds again. "Sorry! Sorry. It's Monique. I gotta answer."

She's crying hysterically. "Come. Over. I need. To talk. To you."

"Okay. You're home?"

"Y-y-yeah."

"See you in a few minutes." I leap up, causing America to topple onto her side. "I gotta go."

She rolls her bright chocolate eyes up at me. "You got women problems, Rafa?"

"Huh? Did you hear Mom say that?"

America's chin slightly bobs. "She won't let you take the car, you know."

"I know." Jesús is at work, Jojo's in our room with a friend playing video games, and Mom is in her room, watching a chick flick she rented. The spare key is hanging on the rack in the kitchen. My hand is on it, thinking I'll just take it and run, but then I decide to go tell her. Not ask—tell. She knows the Sadie's situation, so I won't have to explain a lot.

I knock and open her door. Mom is in sweats, lying on the bed, her hand tucked into a bag of microwavable popcorn, her eyes bright with tears.

"Mom, I'm going to Monique's. I just have to."

"Okay."

"Okay? I won't be late."

"Okay."

It takes me a moment to realize I'm continuing an argument I've already won.

I swing the door shut, then open it again. "Hey, Mom, does it get any easier?"

I think she's paying more attention to her movie than to me, but then she answers, "Only if you're with the right person."

* * *

Monique is a mess, tears carving black rivers into her makeup. Her hair, which was swept up in a fancy do, is now a lop-sided bird's nest. The neckline of her shiny red dress, which plunges dangerously low in both the front and the back, is askew, revealing transparent bra straps. Her matching shoes, with four-inch heels and sharp triangles at the toe, are flung across the carpet, which contains many more brown spots than when I saw it last. She's home alone; she told me her mom and Chad and the rat-dogs are off on a romantic week-end at the coast. They've acquired a white sofa, moved in next to the white baby grand and pinball machine, and Monique, a quivering heap, is slumped onto it. Between jagged sobs, she cusses Luke and his date in long strings of filthy words.

I sit next to her, my hands in my lap. I don't feel like touching her. Vindication wells within me like bile. I can only think *Good! Good! GOOD!*

Obviously she spent hours getting dressed up for another guy, and considering how sexy her look once was, it hardly seems that she was planning to go out with him "as friends."

"How could he do this to me?" she moans.

"Maybe since you broke up, he figured the Sadie's plans were off."

"No! He confirmed our plans on Facebook yesterday. For the whole world to see! He set me up for this—this humiliation. I want to know who she is."

"That's easy." Tor never got back to me, so I text Diego. I wait for the relay of phones among the kids there, before he texts me back the answer. "She doesn't even go to our school. She's from Fresno, a friend of his cousin's."

"Oh!" She pounds her thighs with her fists. "Girls from other schools can't buy tickets for our Sadie's. Luke must've gotten a girl from our school to—shit! Do you see how many people are involved?" She stamps her stocking feet in a frenzied patter. "Oh! I want to scratch her eyes out."

"She probably doesn't know anything about you. She probably thinks Luke invited her to the dance because he needed a date."

She eyes me fiercely. "Whose side are you on?"

"I'm just wondering: Why don't you want to scratch Luke's eyes out?"

"I—I—I do! The way he dissed us both!"

"Not me. The only way I feel dissed is that my girl wanted to go to Sadie's with another guy."

"Rafa, I told you I didn't *want* to. I already invited him, and I couldn't very well—"

"I gotta go," I say, standing.

"Don't leave me. Please, Rafa! Let's me and you go to Sadie's."

I look down at my ragged jeans and hoodie. "I'm not exactly dressed for it."

"You can stop off at home and change. I got tickets. We'll have fun. We'll completely ignore Luke and that bitch."

That doesn't seem likely. "Naw, I don't feel like being second choice—leftovers."

"Oh, Rafa. You know you're my number one. Moldy Muffin is playing, and I've always wanted to hear them. Troy Muffet is really hot!"

"Let's see, you want me as a replacement date so you can see a hot guy."

"I mean on the guitar!" she says in a fluster, her eyes wide with guilt.

"Tor is in that band," I say vaguely.

"Who's that?"

"The girl who sits in front of me in Ms. Becker's class."

"Oh, that freak? You think she can introduce me?"

"I doubt it. You weren't very nice to her." My next words roll off my tongue before I can think through to the end of my sentence. "Guess you'll have to snag your next boyfriend on your own."

"Oh, baby, don't say that!" She leaps up at me, circles her arms around my neck, and pulls me down to her. "I so should've invited you! I hate Luke Jefferson! I love you."

It's what I've been wanting to hear for weeks, but not like this. Not with the name Luke Jefferson in the same breath. She kisses me, but I don't kiss her back.

Her sad eyes look deep into mine. "What?"

"I think hate is a kind of love. I'd like it better if you didn't feel anything for him at all. Just neutral."

"I'm trying to get over him. It's not easy. When you and me started going out, I thought, well, he'll be sorry. He'll come after me, try to get me back."

"Why do I feel like a tool right now?"

"Let me finish! As time went by I realized what a better guy you were, a better person. Nicer. You were—are—so into me. I do love you, Rafa, I do."

"So that's why you didn't invite me to Sadie's?"

"I wanted to make him pay. Feel regret. See what he couldn't have. Because now I'm yours. I could prove it to you. We can spend the whole night together."

She kisses me again. It makes me feel sad and hollow.

"You won't forgive me," she accuses. "You don't love me."

"I forgive you. I love you," I recite automatically. "Rationally, I know that. Physically, I can't . . . I don't feel . . . I'm too angry with you."

"Then we can just get in bed and cuddle." She rubs my chest, searching my face.

"I told my mom I wouldn't be late."

"You could call her and say you decided to spend the night with Diego. I told my mom I was spending the night with Porshia the night me and uh . . . the night I spent at Pismo Beach."

I sigh. Luke again. "She trusts me because I'm a trustworthy person. I don't think I want to change that."

She slaps my arm. "You don't have to go all Boy Scout on me. Don't call, then. She knows where you are, safe here with me."

"Can't. My parents care what I do."

Her eyes narrow. I know I dissed her parents, accidentally on purpose. "Parents? I thought that Mexican guy is just living with your mom. At least Chad has enough respect to marry my mom."

"You shouldn't talk stuff about people you know nothing about. That *Salvadoran* guy cares about us a hundred times more than my own dad ever did."

"Sorry. I didn't mean to dis him. I'm just trying to talk you into staying with me."

"Want me to drop you off at Shelley's?"

"Naw, she'll think it's funny I got stood up. I guess I'll just drink a bottle of Chad's wine and pass out."

I brush her nose with my finger. "Stay away from that two-hundred-dollar bottle, you wino."

She nods and gives me a little smile. She looks exhausted.

"Maybe you should just go to bed. I'll tuck you in."

"You will?"

"Uh-huh." I stand and pick up her shoes, which dangle from my fingers by the heel straps, as light as air.

She takes my hand and leads me upstairs. Her room is

pink with a white lace canopy bed and matching white furniture with gold trim. Clothes, makeup, and junk are piled high all over the place, and her bed is a heap of pillows and blankets. She steps out of her dress and goes into the bathroom. She's in there a long time, the water running in the sink.

I pick her dress off the floor, arrange it on a hanger the way I've seen my mom do, and tuck it and the matching shoes deep into her walk-in closet so she won't have to look at them again tonight. Then I pull all the bedding off the bed, and make it from scratch, turning down one side so she can climb in.

At last she emerges from the bathroom, wearing pink flannel bottoms and a pink T to match, her face scrubbed clean, her hair brushed out, her breath smelling toothpaste fresh. She's far more beautiful this way than she is all done up, but a guy can never convince a girl of that.

She gets into bed, and I smooth the blankets under her chin. "Comfy?" I ask.

"Won't you hold me, Rafa? Just for a little while?"

I take off my shoes and slip under the covers. We hold each other tight, our bodies touching from forehead to toe. Her breath grows deeper and slower. I think she's asleep when she says, "I think I learned something tonight."

"I think I did, too." It has to do with the discussion I had a couple weeks ago with my mom, about love and lust, but I don't tell Monique that. I get up, lace my shoes, and come around to her side of the bed. I watch her face, lashes poised on her cheeks, lips slightly parted. Softly, I kiss her. "Night, princess," I whisper.

"Night, Prince Charming. Love you."

"I love you, too."

I turn off the light and descend the stairs. I let myself out of the house, locking the front door behind me. The pee-pee boy startles me; I wasn't expecting to see another human figure. I have to laugh. It makes me wonder why I'm so happy.

I believe Monique did learn a lesson tonight.

We're one step closer to the way I really want us to be.

Chapter Twenty

Monday morning, five A.M. A knock on the door. I think it might be Jojo, who has stayed out all night wandering around with his homies and now wants back in. Hazy with sleep, I wonder why he doesn't just sneak into our bedroom window like he usually does. I'm at the kitchen door before I'm fully awake, dressed only in boxer shorts and a long-sleeved T-shirt. It's freezing, but I figure I can open the door for Jojo and get back in bed before the covers cool down.

There's another three sharp raps on the door, not at the kitchen door, I realize, but the front. None of us ever use the front door.

A woman's gruff voice says, "Open up. Police."

Don't let him be dead, shot down in some stupid petty crime, please God, let Jojo be alive. I fling open the front door and step back, knocking into someone. I twist around to find Jojo, dressed like me, rubbing the sleep from his eyes, having sprung from his own bed only a couple feet from mine.

It's not the police, but ICE—Immigration and Customs Enforcement—who often misrepresent themselves to get through the door. There's three of them, a young pretty woman, who looks more like a preschool teacher, and two guys, one with muscular arms and the other with a droopy mustache. All of them are Hispanic, dressed for the cold in puffy uniform jackets.

"We're looking for Jesús Castillo," says the woman officer.

"Ain't nobody named that here," says Jojo. "We're the Montoyas and you woke us up in the middle of the night for no good reason."

Jojo doesn't know what he's up against, that they've no doubt watched our house for weeks before attempting an arrest.

"May we have a look around?" asks the woman, in a sweet, high voice.

"Sure," says Jojo. "If you want to waste your time, go ahead."

"No, wait! I'll get our mother," I say, but the ICE officers have quickly stepped inside and shut the door behind them.

"Get out of my house," says Mom, standing in the darkened hallway. Her hair is matted and her robe is askew, falling off one shoulder.

"This young man has invited us in." The ICE lady gestures toward Jojo, and Mom's shoulders slump. "We will need all the residents of this household seated in the living room, please."

Mom gathers our shoulders in her arms and herds us to the sofa. We sit huddled together, her gripping us so tightly it hurts. Both me and Jojo are still, knowing that Mom gains strength by our physical closeness.

"We're all American citizens here, born in this country," says Mom, her chin raised in defiance. "I am Marta Montoya, and these are my sons, Rafael and José Montoya. I can show you birth certificates for us and their little sister, who is sleeping. Please leave before you frighten her. Her name is America. She is learning in school that her name means 'land of the free.'" I notice Mom's careful not to mention America's last name, which is Castillo.

"U.S. citizens are free, but not illegal immigrants who are criminal fugitives," says the woman, who seems to do all the talking. "We are here to arrest Jesús Castillo."

My mom's spine stiffens at the word *criminal*, but she says, "You have the wrong address. There is no one by that name living here."

"That's not what that van parked in your driveway says," says the muscular guy.

"It is a licensed cleaning business," says Mom. "I have kept the books. We have paid the income taxes, every penny we owed we have paid. Six years of tax forms, I can show you."

"Mr. Castillo can surrender, or we can search your house," insists the woman.

"*Estoy aquí,*" says Jesús softly, standing at the entrance to the living room. He's dressed in his best jeans and his Western dress shirt with mother-of-pearl snaps. He holds his cowboy hat in his hands.

"Oh, there you are. Have a seat, Mr. Castillo," says the woman, gesturing toward his own easy chair. "We have an interpreter here if you need one."

When Jesús is seated, he and Mom gaze into each other's eyes, communicating without words. She knows by his clothing that he is ready to be taken away without protest. His steady, placid eyes seem to indicate that Mom should let him go, that cooperation with the authorities is their only option.

The female officer refers to a file she is holding. "You were given a court order to report to an immigration judge in San Francisco on . . ." and she gives a date in April, over twenty years ago.

Jesús waits for the mustachioed officer to translate, then nods. "*Es verdad.*"

"And you failed to appear," says the woman, whose words are interpreted again.

Jesús agrees. "*Sí.*"

Mom leaps up and flings her arms out. "He's not a criminal! He missed his court date because he was working. All he knows is work. Breaking his back, picking strawberries, so you can pour cream on them and slurp them down."

The woman ignores Mom's outburst, continuing her interrogation in her calm monotone. "Failure to appear made you a fugitive, Mr. Castillo, albeit unintentional, a fugitive nonetheless. In twenty years, you had plenty of opportunities to come forward. This, however, is not the major offense. We would never have come after you if you weren't wanted by the Department of Homeland Security."

Mom bends backward and raises her eyes to the ceiling. "Oh, so now he's a terrorist! This poor man? Look at him!"

"A gang member, drug runner, human trafficker, possibly a contract killer," drones the woman, shuffling through her file.

Mom laughs out loud. "I'm telling you, lady, you got the wrong guy."

"A member of Mara Salvatrucha."

"*¡No! ¡Nunca!*" Jesús shouts. Never!

"This cannot be!" says Mom. "I know he is a good man."

"Don't be so sure, ma'am. You think you know somebody, but some of these guys have dark, desperate pasts."

"Not my Jesús," says Mom. "Mara Salvatrucha operates in L.A., and Jesús immigrated to San Francisco. You're making a terrible mistake."

"He's being deported. He'll be on a plane back to El Salvador tomorrow."

The muscular guy removes handcuffs from his belt.

"Wait!" Mom moves into Jesús's embrace, and they look into each other's faces, murmuring in Spanish. They kiss good-bye.

Jesús approaches Jojo and kisses one cheek then the other, both drenched with tears. *"¡Pórtate bien, mijo!"* Be good.

He does not hug or kiss me like he did the others. He shakes my hand, almost coldly. For an instant I think he does not love me, that I have not treated him well enough, and he does not care that he has to leave me. He says, *"Ahora el hombre de la casa eres tú."* You are the man of the house now.

With that, he has made me head of our family.

The muscular officer handcuffs Jesús' wrists behind his back, just as America, in her pink Disney princess nightgown, dashes into the living room. "You're taking my papá away? You can't! You can't!"

"You can go to El Salvador with him, little one," the woman officer suggests.

"I don't want to. I want to stay here in Goldhurst with my mom and my brothers and my papá." America throws her arms around Jesús's waist and begins to cry. He bends to rest his cheek against the top of her head.

Mom gently pries her away and steers her to cling to my waist. "Keep her here." She follows the officers outside to see Jesús off.

America pushes away from me and dashes to the window. Jojo and I follow her. We're in time to see Jesús disappear into a black SUV and be whisked out of our lives.

Chapter Twenty-one

Mom takes the day off work, but we all go to school. What else can we do? America begs to stay with her, but Mom has lots of business to take care of. She e-mails America's teacher, Mrs. Gunnison, to say America might be upset today due to family issues. Instead of just dropping America off like usual, I walk her to her classroom.

Later, in Ms. Becker's history class, I sneak my phone out of my backpack and hide it under my desk to text Diego. "Gotta talk."

"At lunch? S end of quad?"

"Yeah."

Then Monique texts me. "Lunch?"

"Can't," I text back and turn off my phone. Monique won't take no for an answer, of course. She'll text and text me and leave me a dozen voice messages. Soon my phone will be dead because she used up all my minutes. No matter how many times I explain it to her, she can't seem to understand how a prepaid phone works.

When the bell rings, I head out to the quad, searching for Diego. Monique comes rushing up to me, wearing a skimpy red racerback dress, with a regular-strapped zebra-striped bra—not my favorite style. Her hair looks like she didn't comb it when she got out of bed, although she probably spent a lot of time on it. A fresh, raging pink pimple has sprouted right between her eyes. "There you are! Didn't you get my messages?"

"Probably not all of them. Phone's probably dead by now."

"This really sucks. I had to pass behind the auto shop coming to school this morning, and Luke was out there with his friends." She crosses her arms and scowls. "They started laughing and dissing me. It was so humiliating."

"Why didn't you take a different route to school?"

"Because I—I shouldn't have to change my routine just because of that asshole Luke Jefferson. I can go anywhere I damn please. He can't stop me just because—" She looks at my face, which feels like cement and must hold a pretty disgusted expression. She takes my hand. "Come on, baby. Let's get out of here."

"I texted you I can't today."

"Why not? You've got the car, don't you? I know. You don't have any money. It's okay. I can pay." She tries to pull me along, but I don't budge. "You're still mad at me."

I have to think what she means. Saturday night and Sadie's seems a lifetime ago. On Sunday we talked on the phone a couple of times, texted, and flirted on Facebook. "Everything's fine," I try to assure her. Everything *was* fine, until *la migra* ripped a gaping hole in my family.

"No, you're mad. I can tell you're mad or you would have lunch with me."

"I gotta see Diego."

"About what? All the drama that went on between us Sadie's night?"

"Nothing like that." I spot Andy on the other side of the quad, talking with someone behind her, who must be Diego. "I'll call you."

"What am I supposed to do for lunch? Go stand in the cafeteria line by myself, like a loser? What if Luke and his friends see me?"

I love her more than anything, but sometimes she just pisses me off. I walk backward and say, "It's not always about you."

A group of guys comes by, heading toward the lunch line.

"Hey," says Monique, giving them a wide smile. She hugs Philip, then Matt R., then Ryan. I'm not jealous; Monique is always hugging somebody.

I walk to the south end of the quad and say, "Hey," as I approach Andy. Her head twists toward me with a surprised, stricken look on her face, as if I've caught her in a private moment. She steps aside and I see that it's not Diego who is standing behind her, but Tor. I can't remember when I last saw the two of them with their heads together—seventh grade?—and I know in an instant what brought on their reunion: me. They're concerned about me, and they don't even know the worst of it. Andy's features slacken, and I realize that she's mirroring my own expression.

"What has that bitch done to you?" Tor asks.

Diego strides up to us. "Is it Jojo?"

I shake my head. "Jesús."

No one says anything for a long moment.

Finally, Andy gets the nerve. "Deported?"

I nod. They all hug me, long and hard.

After school, Jojo and I hang out in the kitchen, waiting for Mom to come home. When I went to pick him up after school, he was right where he was supposed to be. Now he paces the room, his hands tucked into his armpits, while I sit at the table, my chin in my palm. As soon as I had unlocked the backdoor, America dashed into her room to lie on her bed and cry. We haven't heard a sound from her for a while, so she must have fallen asleep. Me and Jojo don't have much to say to each other, probably because the same question is on our minds that we're afraid to voice. *What if Jesús can't get back into the U.S.?*

A little past five, Mom arrives, carrying a newspaper under her arm. Her face looks worn out and reminds me of a poem by this Emily chick we're studying in American lit: "The Eyes around—had wrung them dry." Mom sets the newspaper on the table, Jojo takes her coat and hangs it in the hall closet without being asked, and I warm her a mug of coffee from breakfast.

When we're all settled at the table, Mom says, "They let me stay with him a few hours in a room where he was being detained. His flight leaves early tomorrow morning."

"Will we ever see him again?" blurts Jojo.

"Of course we will, *mijo*."

"Will we have to move to El Salvador?" he asks.

Mom smiles a little. "No. But I will make a short visit there so we can be married. It's the easiest way for Jesús to return to this country legally."

"When can he come back?" I ask.

"I don't know." She sips her coffee and sighs. "It could take months. Years."

"*Years?*" Jojo shouts.

"A couple, maybe. This is all going to take lots of time and money. It would help if your dad finally grants me a divorce."

"I forgot about *him*," says Jojo.

"I don't get why you're still married," I say.

"Oh, boys, Jesús and I should have taken care of our legal matters long ago, but every time it came up, we thought of the expense, and you know Jesús feared the risk of coming forward. If your dad is not cooperative, I will have to hire a lawyer and take him to court. I'll have to hire an immigration lawyer, too." Mom spreads her fingers and claws through her hair. "Oh! It's all going to be so expensive!"

"Those ICE guys think he's a gangsta," says Jojo.

Mom snorts. "¡Estúpido! Jesús Castillo is a common name. It's a case of mistaken identity. It will all have to be straightened out. ICE doesn't care if they arrested the wrong man. They're just glad to be able to ship off another illegal so people will think they're doing a great job."

"I never heard of that gang they were talking about," says Jojo, "and I thought I knew all the gangs there was."

"You're only thinking of the ones around here," says Mom. "There's hundreds worldwide."

"What did they call it?" asks Jojo. "Mario Salva Trunk something?"

"Mara Salvatrucha," says Mom. "They're big and vicious. I did some research on the Internet today. Mara is Salvadoran slang for 'gang.' Salva stands for El Salvador. Trucha is 'trout,' slang for quick-witted and wise. They got started in the 1980s in L.A. to protect Salvadoran immigrants from other Hispanic gangs."

Jojo's face stretches into a crazed leer. "That would be totally bad if Jesús lived a secret gangsta life."

Mom bats his arm. "Mother of God, José, I will not hear such nonsense in my house. It's a mess, but we'll be better off when it's all straightened out, and Jesús safely returns to us as a legal resident."

"Is that a for-sure thing?" I blurt.

Mom collapses her tense shoulders with an agitated puff of air. "I have to believe it's for sure. We all have to believe it to go on. It won't be easy. I tried to find somebody to take over the office cleaning business today, but no luck."

Jojo and I look at each other. Could we stay up all night cleaning toilets, vacuuming carpets, emptying wastebaskets, then go to school the next morning? No way.

"We'll have to let our clients go," says Mom. "A business we've built for six years down the drain."

"Maybe he can get some of his accounts back when he returns," I say.

"Those people will find someone else. They'll have to. My income isn't much. We'll have to cut back, use only one vehicle, for instance."

"How will we pay for all the lawyers and legal stuff?" I ask.

"Hmm. Take out a second mortgage on the house, if we have to. But Jesús and I have been planning for this day, hoping it would never come, but knowing it might. We've got savings."

"We do?" says Jojo. "I thought we were poor!"

"Poor! You kids don't know what the word means. I know of a family who will suffer through this much more than us."

"Who?" asks Jojo.

I know, but I hadn't thought about them until this moment. "Jesús' family back in El Salvador."

Mom nods. "They're totally dependent on what little Jesús makes at the flea market. Several households—a brother, a cousin, his old folks. Now they will get nothing. I doubt that Jesús can find a job in El Salvador. The unemployment rate is sky high."

Again I feel guilty. I try to picture myself driving Jesús' ghetto van into the flea market and setting up our booth by myself, among the grime, the greasy smells, the Spanish speakers, and I can't bring myself to volunteer. I could do some other work. I could make the supreme sacrifice and give up most of my time with Monique. I clear my throat. I gulp. I speak hoarsely, almost in a whisper, "I could get a job."

Mom smiles. "Thanks for offering, *mijo*. I've thought of that, but for now, let's not make too many changes. My nursing classes start soon, and I'm not used to being a single parent. I think I'm going to need you as my backup around here."

"Mamá!" America dashes into the kitchen and leaps into Mom's lap. She wets the front of Mom's dress as she wails, "I'll never, never see my papá again. *Nunca, nunca.*"

"Hush, now, *mija*," says Mom, rocking her. "Such nonsense. You should be glad for your papá. He's going to get to visit his mother and father, brothers and sisters, and all the old friends he hasn't seen in many long years."

"I don't care about those stupid old people. I want Papá to stay here with us always and forever."

"He's coming back."

"He is? When?" America looks both hopeful and doubtful at the same time. She saw the scary ICE officers barging into our house before morning light, the handcuffs on her dad, the ominous black SUV whisking him off, so how reassuring can Mom be?

"I don't know when, *mija*. In the meantime, you'll have to be very brave. Papá will expect you to be, and I will need your help. Here, blow." She places a tissue over America's nose and she cooperates, drying her eyes once again during this long day. "Now, go look in the refrigerator. See what we can have for dinner."

As America slides off her lap, Mom releases the rubber band on the newspaper and flattens it out before her. "Mother of God!" she gasps, staring at the headlines—FUGITIVE ARRESTED IN GOLDHURST—and a photograph of Jesús' van, the sign on its side legible. Mom glances over at America, who has nearly crawled into the refrigerator, reaching for something far back on the lower shelf.

Jojo and I peer over Mom's arms as the three of us read the article in silence. It names Jesús Castillo as a suspected member of Mara Salvatrucha, possibly guilty of drug running and murder. Mom is described as the common-law wife of Castillo, aiding and abetting a fugitive. Farther down, it mentions Jesús' immediate deportation.

"How can we go to school tomorrow?" Jojo whispers. "The kids will be talkin' smack about us."

"Like you go to school every day," Mom says quietly. "Rafa, please move the van into the garage."

I leap up and take the van keys off the hook. One thing the three of us realize is that America must never know that her birthday present to Jesús led to his arrest.

When I return from moving the van, Jojo is placing left-over chicken on a baking sheet while America is tearing lettuce leaves for a salad. Mom is still staring at the newspaper article. I sit beside her. She taps the paper and says down low, "This is how the media ruins people's lives. When Jesús is exonerated and returns to us, it will only be mentioned in a tiny article on the back page of the local section."

Mom gets up, stalks to the wall phone, and cancels our newspaper subscription. "That's one less expense," she says, and hands the newspaper to me, nodding toward the garage. I go out and bury it deep in the recycling stack.

The calls start coming in. The first one is from a concerned friend offering Mom her sympathy. The second is a nosy coworker Mom doesn't particularly like, asking for all the juicy details, which she can spread on her coffee break tomorrow. Mom gets rid of her fast. The third time the phone rings, I answer it for her. It's a prank caller shouting, "Wetbacks, go home!" I disconnect the phone cord from the wall jack.

"That's another expense we can live without, the landline. I think America is responsible enough to handle a cell phone."

"I am, Mamá," America says excitedly. "I'll use it only for emergencies." She looks at me. "Like if my ride doesn't show or something."

"Don't worry, my country. Your ride will show, always and forever."

A sharp rap on the front door causes Mom's eyes to pop, then roll toward the entryway.

"Maybe they're back to seize our tax returns," she says. "I made copies this morning. You kids stay put."

El hombre de la casa soy yo. "No, Mom, I'll get it." I make a dash for the door, but I feel Jojo, America, and Mom crowding behind me as I fling it open.

There stands Monique, wearing the same red racerback dress with the zebra bra straps and bearing the *Goldhurst Sentinel* like a breastplate. I didn't think she even knows where I live. It's embarrassing to see her here at our shabby house, with Chad's Thunderbird parked in front, one wheel over the curb. She looks painfully out of place in our ghetto neighborhood, like she got lost and needs directions to the upscale side of town.

"Baby," she calls me, right in front of Mom, "so this is why you were so upset today. Why didn't you tell me? Oh, Marta, I feel so bad for you. Life really sucks." She hugs Mom, who stiffens and looks quizzically at me over Monique's shoulder. None of my friends call her by her first name; she thinks it's disrespectful.

I have to grin and shrug. What can I say? "This is Monique."

"Somehow I figured that," says Mom.

"And this here's Jojo."

Monique holds out her knuckles to slam against his. "Hey, baby banger. I've heard all about you."

Mom forces herself to smile, although I know she's pissed off. "I don't know what you've heard, but my son is not in a gang."

Jojo doesn't seem to hear. He's leering into Monique's cleavage, which for him is eye level.

Monique drops on one knee to look into America's face. "I've heard a lot about you, too!"

America's eyes widen. "You have? Like what?"

"Like what a good reader you are, and how smart you are, and how beautiful. My gosh, Rafa goes on about you so much, I feel myself getting jealous!" She grabs the ends of America's braids and swings them playfully. "Have you ever had French braids?"

"I'd like to, but my mom doesn't know how to make them."

"It's easy. I'll show you." She straightens and looks at Mom. "Would that be okay with you, Marta?"

Mom shrugs, not quite as easy to impress as America. "Why not? Straight braids, French braids—what does it matter? I've got bigger concerns."

"Oh, I know!" exclaims Monique, sauntering into the living room without being invited, looking over the worn carpet and shabby furniture with a discerning eye, and finally settling into Jesús' easy chair. "That's why I'm here to the rescue. How's Jesús doing?"

We all follow her lead and take seats in the living room.

"*Mr. Castillo* is as well as can be expected, considering he's being deported tomorrow," says Mom.

"So it's all true. What a nightmare! This is just awful!" says Monique, smacking the headlines with the back of her hand. "Dragging your good family name into this mess. Oh, it makes me so raving mad I want to do something!"

Mom holds up her palms. "I think we've got it covered. Thanks, anyway."

Monique stares at the newspaper a moment, then punches numbers on her cell. She asks for the editor, but doesn't seem to get him. "Well, you tell him these headlines are an outrage. That's what you newspaper guys do, prey on the misfortunes of good, hardworking people! Especially if they're not white. That's how you stay in business. Hurting people, wrecking their lives. You should see what you've done to my mother. You're tearing her apart!" We hear the person on the phone say something, and Monique responds, "Never mind what my name is," and hangs up. She is slightly breathless, her mouth hanging open, a bubble of spittle at the end of her tongue.

"Why thank you, Monique. That was most eloquent," Mom says. I can't tell if she's being serious or sarcastic because I've never heard her use the word *eloquent,* but she bears a broad smile. Maybe it's because a piece of her own mind has been transported to the newspaper, or at least to someone at the newspaper who answers the phone, without her having to make an ass of herself.

Monique moves over to the sofa to sit next to Mom. She arranges Mom's hair, one side behind her shoulder, the other in front. "You need a trim, I think, Marta. In times like these, a girl can't afford to let herself go. Oh! What's this? A few strands of gray! So color, definitely color, and while we're at it we better do some highlights. Have you ever considered henna?"

Mom raises one side of her upper lip. "Isn't that red?'

"Just a touch, to set off those amazing cheekbones."

"Yeah?" Mom grows in her seat, her hands patting her face. "You think?"

"Don't worry, Marta. You can just forget about that gangsta. You'll find a guy way better than him. My mom always does hella fine on rebound, and you're way hotter than her."

That night, while I'm getting ready for bed, Jojo is busy at the computer, poring over images of mean-looking Hispanic guys with their shirts off, wearing rosaries like necklaces. Tats of MS-13 and skulls cover their entire upper bodies, even their faces.

"You think Jesús could've been involved, like long time ago?" Jojo asks.

I nod toward the screen. "He doesn't have tats like that. He doesn't have any at all."

"But this says the gang got started by Salvadorans, trained to fight in the civil war, and Jesús came here to get away from the civil war. He's the kind of dude who would want to protect his own, and that's what MS-13 did."

"Dude, he immigrated to San Francisco."

"They got MS-13 in Frisco. It's all over the place, fifty thousand members. See, our government deports their members back to El Salvador, and those gangstas jump in more dudes, and then they all come back here illegally." Jojo starts pawing through the bottom drawer of his bureau, where he keeps things he collected as a little kid.

"What are you looking for?"

"Nothin'," he says, throwing Happy Meal toys, baseball caps, and soccer team trophies behind him.

"Nothing? Looks pretty important the way you're going at it."

"Nothin'!" He slams the drawer shut on a stuffed giraffe.

Chapter Twenty-two

Mom is at the kitchen table, studying. I'm sitting there, too, trying to read *The Great Gatsby* for American lit. I'm reading words, but I can't put many together to make sense of it. Tomorrow in class when Mr. Espinoza asks if I read, I can honestly say yeah, but like a lot of other kids, I'll add, I didn't understand it. Mostly I'm sitting around trying to keep Mom company. Jesús has been gone over three weeks now, leaving a hollow space in our household that refuses to fill itself in.

Mom leans over a gigantic chemistry textbook, working out a formula. When she studies, she wears her glasses with owl-like, old-fashioned black frames. I wish she'd bust out the money to buy herself some of those hot little rectangular frames all the girls wear, but I don't even suggest it. She's tight about everything these days, especially stuff for herself.

My phone chimes, signaling a new text. I take it out of my pocket, flip it open, and see that Monique wants me to call her. We've got plans to go to the school play, *The Crucible*, tonight. It's extra credit for American lit, but mostly an excuse to be together. What's the point of talking on the phone when I'll be seeing her later?

Mom looks up, obviously interrupted by the sound of my phone. She notices the cover of my book and says, "I remember that one. It's the most romantic book I ever read."

"It is? I can't figure out what's so great about Gatsby. He just throws big parties."

"He's trying to attract Daisy, the love of his life. But she doesn't even notice him because she's in high society and he's from a lower class."

"He sure doesn't act poor. He's got this huge house and car and airplane."

"He's involved in organized crime. You know, there was a lot of that during Prohibition."

"Gatsby is a gangsta? Whoa!"

"Only so he can afford Daisy. He's trying to be someone he's not. And that never works out in a relationship. It has a very sad ending."

Now that I know a little bit more about what's going on, the reading gets easier and the book gets better.

A few minutes later my phone chimes again. Part of the problem is that it's too quiet around here. Funny thing, Jesús is a real quiet guy, but with him gone it's even more quiet. No one speaks Spanish anymore. Surprise, surprise, I miss it. Spanish sounds like home to me; it's warm and funny. That's another thing: no one laughs much around here either. I miss that even more.

"Oh!" Mom exclaims. "Oh! Oh! Oh!" She pounds her forehead with the heel of her hand. "I just don't get it, and I got a test tomorrow. I'm afraid I'm too stupid for this."

"Don't say that."

"It's true. Look." She pulls out a quiz from her folder with a big fat red F on the top. "I didn't get chemistry in high school. I don't know what made me think I could get it now."

"I know you're smart, Mom, cuz America is smart."

"She's got two parents, you know. You boys never gave

Jesús credit for nothing. I can't concentrate since he's been gone. I can't think straight, and I don't have enough time to get all this studying done. Now is not a good time for this." She sweeps her arms over all her books and scattered papers.

My phone starts to chime again, and I talk louder, trying to drown it out. "Yeah? Well, when do you think the clinic is gonna give you another chance like this?"

"I've just been thinking about the clinic. It's open on Saturdays, you know. If I quit school, I could take an extra shift and get paid time and a half."

"Mom, Mom, you're not making any sense. Nurses get paid way more than phlebotomists! Stay in school and we'll be way ahead."

"But I'm not gonna pass chemistry."

"Get a tutor. Try harder. You don't pass, take it again." It's kinda funny, because these are the exact same words she's used on me a hundred times.

Mom pulls off her ugly glasses and takes both of my hands in hers. "Since when have you become so wise, *mijo*?"

I try to speak gruffly, mimicking Jesús without cracking up. "*El hombre de la casa soy yo*, and I say you're staying in school."

"*Bueno, si tú lo dices, hombre.*" If you say so, man.

We laugh together. It's a great moment we're having, but another text message interrupts us.

"It costs us money every time she does that," says Mom. "I hope you've told her."

"I have."

"Well, tell her again."

"Mom, you don't understand. When we're not together, she misses me and I miss her, and like, I know you're working hard at getting Jesús back, and I know you guys e-mail or talk on the phone every week, but—don't get mad or anything—I don't see that you *miss* him all that much."

"*Mijo*, we've been together eight years! When you're that close to somebody, you don't need to be in the same room with him or in contact with him every minute. I feel his love no matter where he is."

I squint my eyes and cock my head. "You're not even tempted to go out on him?"

She shakes her head.

"What if some hot doctor at the clinic started hitting on you?"

She laughs. "Then he'd probably be married."

"What if he was single *and* had a fine truck?"

She laughs even harder.

"What if Jesús is down in El Salvador right now messing around with some cha-cha girl?"

"Cha-cha girl?"

"Whatever."

"*Mijo*, look. When you truly love somebody, there's no one else in the world you can even think of being with."

I sort of believe that, too. I still don't understand why Monique planned to go to Sadie's with Luke, and it still hurts.

Mom glances at her watch, and with a sigh, begins to gather her books and papers.

"Hold it. Don't you have to study for your test some more?"

"I can't. I have to get ready to go to America's school program."

"Oh, that carrot thing is tonight?" For weeks we have been hearing about America's role in *The First Thanksgiving*. The kids in her class are making what they call Friendship Soup, and America is going to be a Native American who places a carrot in the kettle. The way she's been talking about it, you'd think she has the starring role in *High School Musical.* "You keep studying, Mom. I'll take her."

"Oh, I couldn't. I'd feel too guilty. First her father leaves her and then her mother lets her down? No way."

"Mom, it's a matter of her sticking a carrot in a pot. I can watch her do it and tell you all about it. Anyways, I hate the way they hype up friendship between the Pilgrims and the Indians. It was the beginning of the end for those poor suckers."

"You got a point, *mijo.* We'll see if America is okay with it."

Of course America is totally down with it. All the other kids will have boring parents with them. She gets a cool big brother.

Next, I gotta deal with Monique.

"What do you mean, you're standing me up?" she shouts over the phone.

"Sorry, sorry. I forgot I gotta go to America's thing tonight," I tell her, which isn't exactly true. "You don't really want to go to that dumb play anyways. You'd talk and text through the whole thing, and we'd probably get kicked out."

"I want to see you," she says in her pouting way.

"I want to see you, too."

"Does America need me to do her hair? If I can sneak a car, I could come over."

Monique has only been at our house once, which is one too many times for me. "I don't think Indians wore French braids."

We talk a bit longer, then I go into the bedroom to change my clothes and find Jojo on the computer.

"Dawg, check out this MS-13 video. They're totally badass."

I look over Jojo's shoulder at images of corpses, partially covered with blood-soaked blankets, some of them decapitated, with the Mara Salvatrucha tattooed guys standing over them, flashing devil-horned gang signs with their index and little fingers.

"Don't you have something better to do?" I ask, but he's so absorbed, it's like he doesn't hear me. It's then I notice his binder, *MS-13* slashed across it with blue pen in big, bold letters. On top of it is a wooden rosary, handmade by the indigenous peoples of El Salvador. I guess that's what he was looking for in his treasure drawer.

The first Christmas Jesús lived with us, he put rosaries inside the toes of our stockings. We didn't know what they were for and made a game of trying to lasso each other's heads with them. Mom took them away from us and tucked them into our treasure drawers. As far as I know, that's where they've remained until now.

I reach in the closet for a long-sleeved dress shirt and slip on some khaki slacks that I hardly ever wear. Jojo finishes watching the video and says, "Where you going?"

"America's school program."

"The carrot thing? It's like tonight?"

"Uh-huh. I'm taking her. Mom has to study."

In the kitchen, Mom is braiding America's hair. Her costume is made out of a pillowcase dyed brown, with cutout arm- and neck holes and fringes at the hem. She made her necklace by stringing dyed macaroni, and Mom tops her hair off with a feather sticking up at the back of her head.

"All ready to go?" I ask. Just then my stomach growls. "Hey, Mom, what about dinner?"

"We're going to have Friendship Soup after the program," says America.

I eye the precious carrot in her hand, washed but not peeled. She's been carrying it around for days, and it's starting to look a little worn out. Multiply that by all the other vegetables carried around in the grimy hands of her little classmates, and it sort of makes me gag. "Mom! Can't we have money for McDonald's?"

Mom shakes her head. "I'm sure they'll give you plenty to eat. Besides, aren't you hitting the fast food a little too hard these days?" She pokes my gut.

I look down and notice for the first time it's sticking out! I, Rafael Gabriel Javier Montoya, have a pot belly! Mom doesn't mean anything by her teasing, but it hurts. I've always been in shape, and now I feel ashamed. That's doesn't stop me from craving a burger and fries. "Mom, that carrot looks *used*. I don't want to get no diseases."

"You're absolutely right." I think she's headed for her purse to slap a ten-spot across my palm, but instead she takes a fresh carrot out of the vegetable crisper and rubs it vigorously under the faucet. She tries handing it to America. "Here ya go."

"But I've been practicing with *this* one."

"It's all the same," I say crossly, and switch carrots on her.

Schools are weird at night, all black except for the yellow squares of lighted classroom windows. Leading America by the hand down the walkway, I get that old thrill of open houses long ago.

The classroom already smells like soup. The desks have been set in a circle, with a clearing in the center of the room.

There's a fake fire of whirling lights, and a big black pot set on it.

I sit at one of the desks like the other parents and family members, feeling cramped, remembering what it was like to sit in the same classroom all day, waiting for recess time when I could run out and play.

The program is pretty routine. The Pilgrims come in, then the Indians come in, and each one puts a different vegetable in the pot and says a couple of lines. America is one of the better ones because she turns to the audience and delivers her lines in a big, proud voice, a silly grin plastered on her face, and eyes rolled toward the ceiling.

Afterward, it's the kids' job to serve their guests and themselves. They all get in line at the back counter, where there's a couple of Crock-Pots of *real* soup, bread, and pumpkin pie. It seems like a pretty good dinner.

While America and I are sitting there slurping our soup, her teacher, Mrs. Gunnison, comes over to us. She's an older white lady who looks like she should have retired long ago.

"I'm so glad you could join us," she says. "I've been meaning to call home."

From my experience, a call home is never good. It either means a discipline problem or an F, and I wonder if Jesus' absence has been affecting America more than we realize.

"My students took a reading test recently, and America scored at the fifth grade, third month!"

"I know she's a good reader. She's always reading to me."

"But three grade levels ahead! That's rather remarkable, especially for an ESL student."

I'm trying to think of a polite way to tell Mrs. Gunnison that English is not America's second language when she goes on to say, "You can be very proud of your daughter, Mr. Castillo," and shakes my hand.

My hand is still sticking out as she moves on. Daughter? America and I look at each other and smile. I peer around the room, and a lot of the parents do look young, in their early twenties. I know a few kids in my high school who are already parents, but I never thought much about it. If you have a kid at fifteen, you got a second grader at twenty-two! I try to picture Monique in this setting and blink away the image.

Monique would make a terrible mother.

Chapter Twenty-three

Christmas is pretty dismal. I hang a string of colored lights around our house like Jesús usually does. Jojo asks for an iPod and doesn't get it. Mom bakes cutout sugar cookies with America, but I can tell she's rushing through the motions just to get it over with.

My dad has granted Mom a divorce without any problem, and besides getting all her schoolwork done, she's busy meeting with legal advisers, updating her passport, and applying for a visa to El Salvador. It all seems like a big hassle, but Mom told me this is easy compared to clearing Jesús' name of criminal activity, which remains the big snag in their plans. Jesús told her nothing he does on his end seems to advance his case, but he keeps trying to find a way.

The only real holiday fun we have is going to Tía Lupe's house in Reedley on Christmas Eve. It's a tradition for Mom's whole family to get together to make tamales, and I eat more than my share. In January it's a relief to see our town swept clean of Christmas. It's a new year filled with the hope of Mom and Jesús' marriage and Jesús' returning to us as a legal resident.

One Saturday I wake up to an empty house. America has gone to the snowpark in Sequoia with a friend's family, Mom is in class, and Jojo has Saturday school for truancy. I thought that when Jesús got deported, Jojo would help Mom out by behaving himself, but that lasted only a few weeks. Monique isn't around either. She went with her mom and Chad to shop post-holiday sales in L.A.

I decide to go for a run, but I don't know where. I get up, make some toast, and pull on gym shorts and a couple of shirts. I slip my phone in my shorts pocket, then take it out again and slap it on the bureau. A phone can be like a short leash, always tugging you out of the moment and dragging you into places you might not want to go. I don't get much time alone these days and right now I just want to enjoy it.

Outside, the lawns, rooftops, and parked cars are white with frost. It's pretty cold, somewhere in the forties, but I'll warm up fast. We've had a hard, three-day rain and the air is sweet and clear. I can see all the way to the snow-topped peaks of the Sierra Nevada, which are frequently hidden in valley smog. My breath forms a milky cloud, and my legs churn slowly at first, but I feel good.

I pick up speed and go clear across town to the eastern outskirts, running the red lights when there's no cars around and taking the bike trail part of the way. I end up at the new high school, William Saroyan. There's a bunch of cars parked in front of the gym, and that's where I head. I wonder exactly when I knew I was going to end up here. Subconsciously, it might have been before I even got out of bed.

Inside the gym, a wrestling meet between Saroyan and my school, Orange Valley, is about to begin. Steam rolling off me, I stand just inside the door, a bit shyly, as if I'm not sure I'm allowed in, which is a stupid, insecure thought since all meets are open to the public.

"Raaaaaaaafaaaaaa!" Andy yells from across the gym and dashes toward me, dressed in sweats, the top of her wrestling singlet flapping at her waist. She leaps behind me and starts pushing me toward Orange Valley's staging area, rows of chairs set out for the wrestlers to await their matches. I don't have any right to sit there, but Andy presses down on my shoulders until my knees bend, and I'm seated between her and Diego.

"Glad you could make it," says Diego, as if he's been expecting me.

"Who are you wrestling?" I ask.

Diego is hunched over, looking down at the floor between his legs. "I'm not. Didn't make weight. Three-tenths of a pound over."

"Oh man, that sucks! Can't you run around some? Sweat it out?"

"I tried. I don't know what's going on with me. Too much salt yesterday, I guess." He looks over at me with a resigned expression. "It happens. There's always next time."

"Except they're not always here." Andy nods toward three men with clipboards, hovering around Coach Folsom.

"Where are the scouts from?" I ask.

"Pacific University in Oregon, Cal State Bakersfield, and Missouri Baptist," says Andy.

"So you're okay," I say to Diego, knowing he wants to go to UC Davis. Andy, on the other hand, is not the least bit interested in Davis because, like most universities, they don't have a girls' team, nor do they allow girls to wrestle on the guys' team. The scouting is more crucial for her since she's a senior, while Diego is a junior. She runs her little silver wishbone charm across its chain, and I know exactly what she's wishing for.

"You don't always get an offer from your first choice," says Diego. "Sometimes you don't even get accepted into the university."

"You're still okay," I say, knowing he has several backup schools. "Missouri Baptist! Who's even heard of it?"

"Andy has," says Diego. "Lots."

Coach Folsom approaches me with his usual carved-stone expression. I'm certain he's going to kick me out of the staging area, but he claps my shoulder and says, "I'm sorry about your family's trouble, Rafa. That newspaper doesn't know what it's talking about. Jesús is a good man."

"Thanks, Coach." It's not the first time someone has said something like this, but coming from Coach, it means a lot to me. Maybe I've been wrong about him all this time. Maybe he's always been hard on me for my own good.

"I remember when you were just a little tyke, playing every sport on every school team and city league there was. Jesús would be there for you, sitting through every game."

I remember Jesús always working, but now that Coach mentions it, I know that Jesús always supported everything Jojo and I did whenever he had time.

Coach moves on to talk to some of his wrestlers, and since he didn't ask me to move, the staging area is where I stay. Some of the other guys shake hands with me, knock knuckles, or slap palms. It makes me feel better than I have in months.

Since Diego can't wrestle, the main attraction for me is Andy's match. After she removes her lucky necklace she and her opponent, a short, freckled kid, come forward and shake hands. The referee blows his whistle and the match begins. Andy plays a trick, appearing to look over her opponent's shoulder. He's thinking, *Oh, no, I gotta wrestle a girl and she's distracted? I can't make this pin look too easy*, just as he lands on his butt. Andy's shot is quick and strong, and she's two points ahead with the first takedown. Her offensive position doesn't last. The guy hits a switch, then maneuvers a breakdown, smashing Andy to her stomach. Then comes a long struggle, his legs locking hers apart. Both wrestlers' grunts and pants are audible as he manages to turn her back to the mat. He scores a three-point near fall, the referee down on his knees to check that Andy's shoulders are still off the mat as the first period ends.

For the second period, Andy chooses bottom position, sinking to her knees, hands placed in front of her, then sitting back on her feet. As soon as the whistle blows she scores an escape. Her opponent gets a takedown, then maneuvers a ball and chain, throwing his legs around her and reaching under her elbow. They struggle for some excruciating seconds before he is able to pull her back for another three-point near fall. Andy is getting slaughtered. Behind by so many points, it would seem she'd be willing to get pinned and be done with it.

Not our girl Andy. She's on her feet, ready to go for the third period, neutral position, his choice. Her opponent scores two takedowns and another near fall. Why does she do it? I wonder. Maybe girls wrestle for the same reason guys do: the challenge and the hope of a win. Andy escapes, but falls victim to an ankle pick. She's pounded to her stomach again, causing her opponent to score another takedown before the buzzer. The referee holds high the freckled kid's arm. Utterly exhausted, Andy offers the guy a limp handshake, then shuffles off the mat.

Tears flood her eyes, not because of defeat, but pain. She really took a beating. I want to dash up to her and hold her in my arms, but that's not what she needs right now.

"You held him off," Coach says, swinging an arm over her shoulders. He begins to murmur instructions about how she could have improved her performance.

When she returns to sit with us, Diego points under his nose, and says, "Hey, you got a booger, a big green one."

"Shut up," she says, breaking into a grin. She swipes at her nose with her forefinger, then backhands Diego's shoulder.

He cringes, yelling, "Eeew! You got it on me."

She laughs, causing the tears barely contained by the rims of her eyes to spurt onto her cheeks.

It's a funny exchange, and I'm laughing too. It makes me realize how comfortable Diego and Andy are with each other, how they always act just like themselves, knowing each will be accepted by the other. I always think before I react to Monique, and then I worry how I'm coming off to her. Sometimes I catch myself trying to be someone I'm not, trying to second-guess which someone would be most appealing to her. I wish I could cut that crap out, but the fear of losing her is too great.

The scout from Pacific runs his pencil down our roster, which is clamped to his clipboard, and asks Coach, "Which one is Rafael Montoya? Didn't he make weight today?"

I don't believe it! A recruiter is actually interested in me, and now I have to tell him I *quit* wrestling?

Coach nods toward me. "Academic probation."

It's not exactly true. I quit before I became ineligible. Semester grades will be out soon, and I expect a 3.5, the highest GPA I've had since elementary school. These past couple months, while keeping my mom company at the kitchen table, I decided I might as well get my own work done.

The recruiter shakes my hand. "I saw your performance at the state championships last year. Mighty impressive."

All I can do is gulp the word thanks.

"I got you down as a junior, right? Our one-hundred-forty-nine-pound man will be graduating next year. We'll be looking for a guy to fill his spot on our lineup." He scribbles something next to my name. "Don't worry about academic probation. Happened to me my sophomore year in college. Nothing to be ashamed of. Get some help in your studies, work hard. I'll be keeping my eye on you." He gives me a thumbs-up. "See you next year."

So I still have a chance. If Coach will take me back, I have a chance.

It's Andy who makes the big splash in *Goldhurst Sentinel* headlines. Missouri Baptist University offers her a full-ride scholarship to wrestle on its *women's* team. There's less than a dozen women's collegiate wrestling programs in the country, recruiting from about five thousand girls who wrestle in high school. "Ironically, girls who come from high schools without a girls' program have an edge," the recruiter told the newspaper. "Andrea Kent is a tough competitor with years of experience." The article goes on to say she has a 4.25 GPA, she sings in the top choir, and is active in community service through Key Club.

I'm real proud of her, and sorry too, that I haven't given her enough credit. I thought she was wrestling just to get attention, when it turns out she's as serious about it as any guy. More serious.

After the Orange Valley–Saroyan meet, I start showing up for wrestling practices. At first I just hang out on the sidelines watching, but then Coach asks me to help roll out the mats and sanitize them. Next thing I'm warming up with the team, then participating in the complete practice. It's kind of weird because I don't really know if I'm back on the team or not. I don't even care. I'm just happy to be working out again. This time around, I'm wrestling for all for the right reasons.

* * *

Of course there's somebody who isn't too happy. One Sunday afternoon when Monique and I hang out at Shelley's by ourselves, watching TV, I'm thinking that we could be fooling around in the back room, but it's plain that she isn't in the mood. She's spent the night here and is still wearing her penguin-printed flannel pajama bottoms and a Raiders T-shirt, mainly because I hate the Raiders. The dirty diaper smell never completely leaves this place, and there's leftover plates of food on the coffee table that have been there so long, mold is growing on them. Monique has a box of Red Vines in her lap, which she offers me.

"No thanks," I say. "I've got almost ten pounds to lose."

"I don't want you all scrawny. You quit wrestling, remember? You said it was a stupid sport."

"I never said it was stupid. I said it was unpopular."

"Unpopular. That's it. Who would want to do something unpopular? Go out for football next year. That'd be hot, and you could bulk up." She offers me the candy again.

I ignore the gesture, even though my mouth waters. "I don't like to play football."

"Go ahead then, be a wrestler. If you're so busy wrestling, I might have to find someone else to be with."

She knows words like that make my blood boil, but I try to act cool. "There you go, again. Threatening me."

"I'm just saying, I get bored, always by myself."

I feel a real fight coming on, and I'd like to avoid it, but I just can't help having my say. "You don't think anything is worth doing, so you don't want me to do anything either."

"When did I say nothing was worth it?"

"You don't like school. You don't like sports. You just like sitting around here."

"You like sitting around here, I notice. This is usually

where we end up because you don't have any money to take us anywhere."

"Actually I hate it here. Actually it makes me gag." I stand and start collecting the disgusting leftovers off the coffee table. I run warm, soapy water in the sink, do the dishes, and take the overflowing garbage out to the trash bin. I'm so used to looking around our house for what needs to be done and then doing it that it's sort of a habit. Cleaning house isn't fun, but it feels like kind of an accomplishment. It's way better than doing nothing at all.

Chapter Twenty-four

Sunday morning, five A.M. A knock on the door. Am I dreaming of the morning ICE took Jesús away?

No, Jojo's bed is empty. Circling blue lights race around our room.

I leap up and go answer the door. A stiff, squat police officer is standing on our porch. One we know, Diego's brother Ramón.

Mom, in her robe and pajamas, pushes me aside and places her hands lightly on his forearms. "Ramón! Is he dead?"

"No, but he's arrested."

Mom sort of leans into him, her knees buckling, and he catches her and holds her. After a moment, she balances on her own feet again. "What's he done?"

I notice she doesn't say "accused of," maybe because she's talking to a family friend.

"Vandalism. Over in one of the model homes in that new subdivision, Royal Oak Ranch."

I feel my heart pound as my mind flashes on Monique and me hanging out illegally on the very same property. Was I crazy? Ramón could very well have had to report my arrest to Mom.

"Are you sure it was Jojo?" asks Mom.

Ramón nods. "We caught him and two of his buddies in the act. You'll need to come down to the station."

After he leaves, I get dressed and meet Mom in the kitchen. "Rafa, you'll have to stay here with America."

"He's my brother. I'm coming."

I peek between the blinds and see old Mrs. Tanner across the street, peering out her kitchen window, watching the action over at our house. The yellow light behind her seems to be on at all hours of the night, like she doesn't sleep much, always keeping her eye on her neighbors' business.

"I'll go get Mrs. Tanner," I say.

"*Mijo,* she'll go through our drawers!"

"What do we have to hide? All our business is spread across the front page of the newspaper."

After securing Mrs. Tanner as a babysitter, we head for the police station. I drive while Mom sniffles into a tissue.

"Don't baby him," I say.

"I'm not going to baby him." She blows her nose loudly. "There. All done crying. I'll be as tough as nails." Then she breaks down again.

At the station, a cop shows us into an interrogation room. Jojo is seated there across from a plainclothes detective, who is taking notes on a laptop. At the sight of Mom, Jojo jumps up from his seat to hug her, but she holds up her palm and motions him to sit down again, her eyes red but dry.

The detective is an elderly white guy with white hair and rippling lines across his forehead. He introduces himself as Detective Warner. On the computer, he shows us photographs of the model home me and Monique sneaked into. The walls and carpets of the living room and bedroom are covered with MS-13 gang signs, spray-painted in blue.

Mom glares at Jojo. He drops his head and silently weeps.

"We're especially concerned about this," says Detective

Warner, "because we haven't had any activity of this gang in this area. MS-13 stands for *Mara Salvatrucha*, in case you aren't aware. The members are predominately from El Salvador. We searched the crime scene and found this hidden between the nightstand and bed." He holds up the knit rainbow cap Monique left behind. "We've run a lab on the fibers and indeed it's made in El Salvador. José refuses to tell us where he got it."

"That's cuz I never seen it," says Jojo, swiping at his tears.

"Why didn't you tell Detective Warner you got it out of a box in our garage?" Mom asks him.

"Cuz I never seen it."

"Why would you lie about something so silly?" She explains to Warner, "My fiancée sells these at the flea market."

"Strange that he won't admit to something so small when at the same time he brags his father is affiliated with Mara Salvatrucha in L.A."

"His *father*?" Mom exclaims.

"Yes." Warner nods toward the computer. "We've run a search, and there's no known Mara Salvatrucha member by the name of Hector Montoya in our database."

"No?" Mom smiles ruefully. "Well, maybe you guys shouldn't have put such wild ideas into my son's head."

Mom gets the response she's going for. The detective's eyes pop, and he presses his fingertips against his chest. "Us?"

"She means the authorities in general, ICE in particular," I explain. "And Jojo means our stepdad, or at least he's like a stepdad, the only guy who's been a father to us. He got deported to El Salvador recently, charged as a Mara Salvatrucha member. He's not, though. He's a really good guy."

"I remember reading about that in the paper," says Warner. "What is his name again?"

"Jesús Castillo," I say.

Warner punches his name into the computer. "Ah, here he is."

Mom casually leans closer to the screen to peer into the face of an angry man, about Jesús' height and age, covered in tattoos.

"Says this Jesús Castillo died May ninth of last year, shot and decapitated by his own gang. They'll do in their own, you know, if a member tries to leave them."

My mom's face glows from within. It's the best news we've had in months. Finally our Jesús will be exonerated. With lowered lashes and a raised chin, she says, "You guys and ICE really ought to share your information a little more often."

He shakes his head. "We try, ma'am."

"Try harder," says Mom.

When the detective asks if she wants to arrange Jojo's bail, she says, "No. I think he needs a night in jail to think things over."

"Mama!" cries Jojo. "Do you hate me?"

"Do you hate us?" she asks sternly.

I'm proud of her for standing up to his whimpering.

Detective Warner tells Mom the estimated cost of the vandalism. Divided among the three boys, our share is around ten thousand dollars. He goes on to say that the cost could probably be reduced to a couple thousand if Mom is willing to place Jojo in the county boot camp for juvenile offenders for several months.

Mom stares coldly into Jojo's eyes. "I'll think about it."

On the drive home, she is more angry than sad. "All the

expense of Jesús' deportation and now this! Your brother has ruined us! Now we will have to take out a second mortgage."

"No, we don't. Let's send him to that boot camp."

"*Mijo,* I wouldn't think of it. Jojo isn't that tough."

"If he's tough enough to trash that house, he's tough enough for boot camp. Come on, Mom. He's been getting away with murder his whole life. Maybe it'll teach him something."

Mom starts to cry again and murmurs in a small voice, "He still sucks his thumb."

"Don't I know it? I'm the one who has to listen to him slurping when I'm trying to get to sleep."

"No, no. It isn't possible. I couldn't do it to him."

"I'll do it, then. *El hombre de la casa soy yo.*"

"Oh now, wait a minute, Rafa. Jesús didn't mean you were to decide such weighty matters."

"He meant exactly stuff like this. He knew you'd be too soft on Jojo if he got into trouble. You think Jojo would've pulled this crap with Jesús around? He wouldn't dare."

"He's your brother, Rafa. Your baby brother."

"He's a punk and he needs to be straightened out before it's too late for him. He's going to that boot camp, Mom." I say it again, just because I like the sound of it: *"El hombre de la casa soy yo."*

Chapter Twenty-five

I'm making sandwiches with real deli oven-roasted turkey, lettuce, and tomato. I've got sparkling cider. It's not exactly wine but I know Monique likes it, and Mom is letting me borrow two wine glasses. I've got chips, cookies, cloth napkins, a blanket, and all the stuff.

It's a perfect Saturday in March. We're going to a park near Monique's house. It's our fifth-month anniversary. Five whole months! It's real. It's true love.

I hear someone's rushing footsteps in the hall, and I think it's Jojo. He's been at boot camp six weeks now, and I still expect him to burst into a room. I miss the little jerk, more than I ever thought. Our house feels so empty, just me, Mom, and America rattling around. It's too quiet, too tame. I can't wait until it's back to all five of us again, fighting over who gets the last piece of chicken or the first shower.

It's Mom in the hall, dashing around collecting her books, purse, and sack lunch, before her car pool arrives to take her to nursing school. "You're sure you know how to get to Sonya's house?" she asks.

"Mom, I've dropped America off there before."

"Pickup is four o'clock sharp. Don't get so *busy* with Monique you forget. We don't want to wear out America's welcome there. Sonya's mom has been awfully nice to her since—"

"I know, Mom, I know. Can I have ten bucks?"

"What for? You're packing a lunch!"

"For whatever. Everything costs. Come on, Mom. I'm broke."

"You shouldn't have gotten that expensive deli turkey. The packaged kind is good enough." She slaps a five-spot across my palm. Her cell rings, and she fishes it out of her purse and answers it. "Oh, that's too bad!" she exclaims. "Do you think his arm is broken? . . . Of course, get it X-rayed. . . . Of course, I understand. I'd invite the girls over here, but I got class."

I freeze, thinking, oh, crap. This can't be happening.

Mom finishes her conversation and looks at me. "Sorry, *mijo*. Sonya's brother just had a skateboarding accident and they gotta take him to emergency."

"Mom! Do you know what this means? It's our five-month anniversary. I've been planning this for a week. This is our special celebration, just the two of us."

A horn honks from our driveway.

"Work it out, Rafa. It's the way things are. That poor kid. I hope his arm isn't broken." Mom shuts the backdoor on her "Bye" and is gone.

I should text Monique and warn her America is coming with us, but I'm afraid she'll get pissed and refuse to join us. I stare at the romantic picnic basket packed with loving care. Crap. I unwrap the sandwiches, take some of the meat out of each one, and make a sandwich for America.

I coach her on the car ride over to Monique's. "Try to give us some time alone, okay?"

"I want to be with Monique."

"You can be with Monique. We'll eat together."

"We'll have to feed the ducks together, too. Mom says I could fall in the pond and drown."

"Okay. Just play on the playground for a while first, okay?"

"So you can make out?"

"America!"

She nearly slides out of her seat belt in peals of giggles, and I gotta laugh, too.

When I pull up to the curb in front of Monique's house, she comes running out, dressed in a dazzling yellow halter dress and gold flip-flops that match her huge crescent-shaped bag. I get out of the car to greet her, but America is way ahead of me, bounding up the driveway. Monique slows her pace and her wide smile fades. America doesn't notice, taking her hand and chattering as she leads her to the car. They've only seen each other about three times, but America is always excited to be with Monique, the pretty, big sister she's never had.

Over the top of America's head, Monique scowls at me.

I shrug. "A change of plans."

America jumps into the backseat.

I dash around the car, shouting, "Happy anniversary!" When I kiss her, her mouth doesn't move beneath mine.

"Doesn't she have a little friend we could leave her with?" she whispers.

"We'll have fun. You'll see." I open the car door for her with a sweep of my arm and a deep bow, but I can't even get her to crack a smile.

When we get to the park, America runs to the playground and jumps on a swing. Monique plops on a park bench, crosses her arms, and glares at America. "Kids screw up your life. I'm getting my tubes tied."

I'd like kids someday. Doesn't she even care what I think? I don't try to argue, because when she gets into one of her moods, there's no talking her out of it.

"There's nothing to do here," she complains.

"We could feed the ducks. I brought some stale bread."

She looks at me, one side of her upper lip raised. "I'm not a four-year-old. Let's rent a paddleboat."

"I just got enough to pay for you."

"Just me? I don't want to go alone. Who would pedal? How much you got?"

"Just a five."

"We need money."

I wish I had a job. When Mom told me she wanted me to help around the house rather than earn extra money, I knew things would be this way with Monique. Yesterday when we went to pay for our drinks at Starbucks with Krystal's American Express card, the cashier canceled our order and kept the card, claiming it was invalid. I figured that meant Krystal had reported it as stolen, since Monique was putting so many extra charges on it, but Monique said this often happened to her mom when she gets behind on her payments. Then she has to find a different bank to issue her a new card.

An arc of blue sky hovers over the park. The ducks and geese float by on the pond. Almond-tree blossoms drift like falling snow. None of it costs a penny. I could be happy just sitting here, soaking up the sun and holding hands with the girl I love. If only she were happy, too.

"Pervert." Monique glares at a man who enters the playground and sits on a bench. He's a bearded white guy, about forty or fifty, hunched over in a long coat, even though it's a warm day.

"He seems okay to me."

"Do you see him with a kid? No. He came here to watch the little girls. Or little boys."

"He just looks sorta lonely."

"Hey, I got it!" She smiles so sweetly, my heart lifts. She leans into me, and it's a relief to hold her.

"You got what, baby?"

"How we can make some money."

America runs up to us, asking, "Can we feed the ducks now, Rafa?"

"You were going to play on the playground for a while, remember?"

"I already did."

"It's okay," says Monique. She shifts away from me and pats the bench between us. "Sit right here, America. Let's make you some French braids." Monique digs in her purse for a comb and brush and goes to work on America, smoothing her long hair until it shines. I kind of wish America was not between us, the center of attention, but Monique is finally smiling, and if she's happy, I'm happy. I lean my elbows on the table behind me, lift my face to the sun, and close my eyes, listening to America and Monique's chatter.

"You should really change your name, girlfriend," Monique says.

"I like my name," says America.

"I don't mean your whole name. I mean get a nickname. How about Merrie? No, that's no good. Sounds like Mary. I know. Amy. Amy's not bad."

"I like America."

"I do, too," says Monique. "But it's not cool. You need something short."

"Okay, Mo!" says America, and even Monique has to laugh at the idea of being called that.

They begin discussing celebrities and their hairstyles. I must have dozed for a minute, because now they're on to another subject.

"See that man over there, America?"

"Yeah."

"That's my uncle Bob."

"It is?"

"Uh-huh."

"Want to go over there and say hi to him?"

"Okay."

I open my eyes. America's hair is done up in neat new braids, tracking the slope of her head. Both girls are looking over at the bearded guy in the long trench coat. America jumps up and holds out her hand to Monique.

"No, you go first. I'll be right behind you. Say, 'Hi, Uncle Bob,' and jump in his lap."

"What?" I say.

Monique puts her arm around America and talks directly to her, ignoring me. "He'll have a surprised, happy look on his face, then I'll snap your picture on my cell and e-mail it to my auntie Liz. 'Here's my boyfriend's beautiful little sister,' I'll write. They've been asking for a picture of you."

"They have?"

"Uh-huh. They'll just love it."

America looks across the playground at the man and ducks her chin into her throat. "He's a stranger."

"No, he's not. He's my uncle Bob!"

"You never said you knew the guy," I say.

"Go on, Amy, I'll be right behind you."

"I don't want to be Amy. I'm America. I come from North America and Central America. Two Americas."

"So your parents come from two countries. Big deal. You don't have to have such a dumb name."

"Not two countries, two Americas! Don't you know nothing?"

Monique gives her an impatient push. "Go on. Go say hi to Uncle Bob."

America's lower lip juts out, but she snaps her head forward and begins walking across the playground.

"Monique—" I begin.

"Shhh! Here's the plan." She snuggles next to me and whispers, "Now don't get all weirded out on me. This will work. As soon as I snap the picture, you run up and accuse him of molesting your little sister."

I rear back to get a better look at her face. "You're kidding. What if your uncle doesn't think it's funny?"

"He's not my uncle, tard. We'll threaten to have him arrested. He'll pay us not to. We could get fifty, maybe a hundred bucks off him."

Inside I feel a sort of sliding sensation, like my heart, my lungs, and all my vital organs pool into a quivering heap in the pit of my gut. "You're not kidding."

"Hell no. It's a brilliant idea. He already looks guilty."

"My sister!"

America is halfway across the playground. I leap to my feet. Monique yanks my hand with both of hers, knocking me off balance.

"Not yet! It's not gonna work unless she goes over there by herself first."

I take one last look at Monique. Creamy brown thighs. Beautiful breasts riding high in the blazing yellow halter dress. Full pillow-soft red lips. I avoid her eyes. Inside those eyes lives a horrible person.

Legs and arms pumping, I sprint to America and swoop her up into my arms. "It's just a joke, my country! A bad joke!"

I whirl her around, and she stretches out one arm and

drops her head, shrieking, "Ha-ha! I fell for it," never realizing the danger or the betrayal.

I set her down, take her hand, and walk back to our table. I avert my eyes from Monique, catching only a glimpse of her toenails painted pearly pink, the baby one just a dot. I pick up the picnic basket and steer America toward the car. Over my shoulder, I hurl words in Monique's direction, "You go sit on Uncle Bob's lap. I think he's your type."

"Rafa, where are you going?" she hollers after me. "Rafa, you shit! You can't just leave me!"

"I can."

Finally I can.

Chapter Twenty-six

The rush I get stalking away from Monique lasts all of five seconds. We get to the car, and I unlock the passenger side. I try to push America into the car, but she won't budge.

"Why are we leaving so soon? I was having fun."

I pick her up and toss her in, too roughly. "We're going to another park."

"This is the only one with ducks."

I slam the car door, go around to the driver's side, and start up.

America tries to look back to where Monique is still seated. "How come Monique isn't coming with us?"

"We broke up."

"You broke up? When? How will she get home?"

"She's getting a ride from Uncle Bob," I say, and howl at my own sick joke, which America couldn't possibly get. I'm numb. I set out to enjoy the most romantic day of our relationship and—*poof*—it's gone. Over. At the first red light, I lean over, press my hands against my stomach, and squeeze my eyes shut.

"You got morning sickness, Rafa?"

"Huh?"

"Well, it's the morning and you're sick."

"Boys don't get that."

"You sure? How come just girls do?"

"Ask Mom."

"Is it about sex? You always tell me to ask Mom when something's about sex."

"America! You're killing me!"

"Just asking," she says in a small voice, rolling her eyes from me to her lap. "Do you think you and Monique will kiss and make up?"

"No."

"But I liked her."

"Me too. Too much, though." Too much to see who she really is.

I'm heading toward the park that's behind my high school, across the street from where I usually park. When I get there, I drive right past it. I'm too stirred up to just sit around.

I cruise through the nearby neighborhood. I'm not sure if I can find Tor's house; I haven't been there since the fifth grade. I don't know why, but after fifth grade, boys had all-boys birthday parties and girls had all-girls parties, except for hookup parties in middle school. I'm not sure if Tor is the right person to talk to about this—maybe she'll just laugh in my face—but I'm desperate to talk to someone.

I find her street and then her house, remembering that it's white with a red door. I cut the engine and tell America, "Wait here. I'll be right back."

She crosses her arms in a huff. "Oh hell, I shoulda brought my book."

I shake a finger at her. "Watch that cussing, *hermana*."

I walk up to the porch and ring the doorbell. Tor's little sister answers it and yells back into the house. "There's a boy out here to see you."

Tor appears at the door. "Oh, hi, Rafa." She's in a purple bathrobe, her hair up in a high ponytail, and her face covered with some light green, creamy stuff.

"Do you want to have a turkey sandwich with me?" My voice comes out a little quivery. I hate to beg, but I add, "Say yes."

She peers at me out of two round peepholes. "I'm supposed to leave this cucumber mask on for thirty minutes."

"Wash it off now, okay? I'll buy you a new one."

"You don't have any money. It's supposed to make my skin extra smooth."

"I didn't know anarchists cared about stuff like that."

"My dear boy, don't be stereotyping me. Give me a minute."

She's leaves me standing on the porch, then soon returns, dressed in jeans and a tie-dyed peace T-shirt, her swirly eyebrows drawn on, her face glowing.

"Hey, I think that green stuff is working already," I say.

She laughs. "I don't have much time. I've got something in like an hour."

"This won't take long."

We drive to the park, and while America plays on the playground, I tell Tor what happened. Putting into words what Monique did and speaking them aloud, especially to Tor, makes it seem even worse. She doesn't call Monique insulting names like I expected she would. She doesn't say anything, just listens.

"Now I feel awful," I say. "I still love her and I still want her, but at the same time I don't want her, and I'll never forgive her."

"Well, let's see. Her scheme wouldn't have put America in any real danger."

"But it was so creepy. Right then, I felt I had to choose between her and my little sister. That sad, old guy! It would have been a sick thing to do to him."

She nods. "It's blackmail."

"I knew all along her values were screwed up. So why does this feel so different?"

"I guess you realized how far she'd go."

A thought is creeping into my head. "That's it! America really looked up to her, trusted her, and Monique was willing to throw her to the dogs. Tell me she's a horrible, nasty person, and I should never have anything more to do with her."

"She's a horrible, nasty person, and you should never have anything more to do with her," she says, not even coming close to cracking a smile.

America approaches us, complaining she's hungry, so she, Tor, and I eat the sandwiches I made for Monique and me. The more I eat, the bigger bites I take, rummaging into the basket for the other food Tor lists the books she liked when she was America's age.

She glances at her watch and says, "Oh! I've got to get back!"

"Yeah, right. Thanks for listening. Sorry about your cucumber mask. I'll buy you a new one, I promise."

"My dear boy, you're more important than all that." She runs the back of her hand against her cheek. "Maybe I'm getting too vain."

When we return to Tor's house, a guy is waiting on the porch. "Troy's here already," she says. "Come on, I want you to meet him."

I think to say something like I don't want to take up any more of your band's practice time, but instead I follow Tor up the walkway.

Troy Muffet is slumped on the porch swing in black skinny jeans, his studded belt about mid-thigh, his mop covering his face. At first he doesn't stir, engrossed in a *CosmoGirl* magazine. Cool guys read *Cosmo*? I guess they don't care what looks cool and what doesn't. I guess that's what "cool" is.

"Sorry I'm late," Tor calls out to him. "Rafa needed to talk."

"Your mom told me." Slowly, reluctantly, Troy sets down the magazine. He unfolds his long, lanky body and ambles down the steps, his hair still swinging before his face.

"So Troy, Rafa. Rafa, Troy," says Tor.

"Man." He sticks out a fist to knock against mine, flipping back his hair to reveal a chiseled, handsome face, free of piercings and tats, as clean-cut as a football player. So that's what all the girls have been raving about. "Get everything worked out?" he asks.

"Ah, it's going to be a long time before I have it all worked out. Like, you know, I got to work some girl out of my system. But Tor helped a lot."

"Yep, she's something, isn't she?" Troy embraces Tor from behind, his square chin coming to rest on the top of her head, and I see now that it's not the cucumber mask that has set Tor's face glowing. They're a couple—freaky Tor and this hot guy. Of course, I've known how great Tor is since the third grade, but I never expected a guy like Troy Muffet to figure it out. He must really have it all: looks, musical talent, *and* smarts.

We say our good-byes, then I begin the drive home with America. I wonder if Monique hates me for leaving her at the park. She must've walked home or gotten a ride. Maybe she's sorry for what she did and wants to apologize, and I'll apologize for driving off without her. From now on every time she does something bad, like dissing a teacher or stealing, I'll tell her it's wrong and not to do it, and she'll learn to do what's right and be a better person.

But if I want her to change so much, how can I say I truly love her? Loved her? Love her? I don't know!

At home I check my e-mail. Nothing from Monique. I check our family's e-mail, and there's something from Jesús. He doesn't have a computer, but at least once a week he makes it to an Internet cafe. He has enclosed a photo of three men standing out in front of his parents' shabby house, leaning against a broken-down car. I wonder why he sent the photo because I don't know any of the men. Then I see it: the little, skinny guy on the right with the drawn, hollow-cheeked face is Jesús. He looks so weak and hungry it's hard to believe he's the same man we said good-bye to just five months ago.

I log onto Monique's Facebook wall, not really thinking, just doing it out of habit. I read the message "Monique only shares certain information with everyone. If you know Monique, add her as a friend." She unfriended me! The biggest dis there is! She didn't unfriend Luke Jefferson, not even after the Sadie's fiasco. She must really hate me.

That night I hardly sleep at all. I keep checking my phone for a text or a message from Monique. I delete her number from my phone to keep from calling her in a weak moment, but that doesn't do me any good either. I've got her information memorized.

I wake up to a whole empty Sunday. I've got to do something to keep the ache from burning a hole clean through me.

I head out into the garage and start loading Jesús' van with merchandise. I've been taking the van out every week or so since he's been gone, so it starts up just fine. I head to the flea market like I have hundreds of times with Jesús. It's been over five months since I've been here, but it's like I haven't missed a week. Everything is the same: the tires, T-shirts, CDs, live birds. The smell of chilies, tacos, churros. The raucous salsa music. The whirling colors of piñatas and flags. Site No. 124 stands empty, waiting for me to back in.

This early in the morning, with most people still at church, business is slow. The regulars, Jesús' old friends, including Carmen the purse vendor next door, approach me and ask about him in Spanish.

"El nombre de Jesús Castillo es bueno." The name of Jesús Castillo is good, I reply, to explain that his name has been cleared of all criminal charges.

It doesn't matter that my Spanish is lame; Jesús' friends understand me. They clap my shoulder, shake my hand, laugh with relief, and tell me that they never doubted Jesús' character for a moment. He is a man of honor, a good friend.

They press me for more information, and I say, *"Mi madre viajará a El Salvador. Ella y Jesús se casarán, y él volverá a este país legalmente."* My mother will travel to El Salvador. She and Jesús will be married, and he will return to this country legally.

This news is received with more backslapping and congratulations. Of course their next question is *"¿Cuándo?"* When? is the big question that no one can answer. It's not certain Jesús will ever be able to return to this country, but today, I have nothing to share with his friends but hope.

Customers begin to trickle then pour onto the sunny, dusty flea market grounds. A woman approaches my booth and begins to finger one of the crochet manteletas. My heart pounds a bit faster: stage fright. She looks like she speaks only Spanish. Sure enough, she begins to ask questions in Spanish, and I answer them in Spanish. I think of how I would say something in English, then think of which Spanish expression I know that is closest to the English meaning. It sort of hurts my head, but I do just fine. I make a sale.

After that, I sit in my folding chair behind my table of displayed wares, but no customers approach me. I ask Carmen to keep an eye on my booth, then stroll through the grounds just for something to do. I freeze, one foot ahead of the other, my heart trying to burst out of my chest. A girl is walking in front of me in tight cutoffs, black hair streaming down her back. It's Monique. What do I do? What will I say? It's not Monique— too tall. With a shudder, I breathe deeply and move on.

Other vendors, I notice, are standing before their booths, hawking their wares, drawing customers in. When I get back to my booth, that's what I do, in English and in Spanish.

Business picks up. By the end of the day, I've made over two hundred dollars to send to Jesús in El Salvador, and a few bucks for my own pocket. My jaw aches, my tongue feels swollen, my mind is weary. I realize I've been speaking Spanish most of the day.

At some point there's a lull in Carmen's business, and she takes the opportunity to saunter over to my booth to make her usual offer. "Have I got the girl for you, *guapo*."

Throughout the day, I think I've spotted Monique three different times, and yet whole minutes have gone by without my even thinking of her. "Thanks anyway," I tell Carmen. "I'd rather choose my own girl."

Even though I suck at it.

Chapter Twenty-seven

By the time Mom's trip to El Salvador comes up, school is nearly out and Jojo has been released from boot camp. It's not Doña who stays with us for the week; it's Grandma Letty. She hasn't seen us for about four years, and she says she misses us. The plan is for my dad to drive her up to Goldhurst from L.A., and I'm nervous about seeing him. It turns out to be no big deal. His paunch hangs farther over his belt and his hair is thinner. When I shake his hand, he seems nothing more than a family friend who hasn't been around for a while. He complains to me that now that he is officially divorced, he has no good excuse not to marry his own longtime girlfriend, Doreen.

While Mom is away, I plan a surprise for Jesús, a sort of homecoming gift for whenever he does get back. I find out the name of the friend of the friend of Mom's who painted the sign on his van and have it redone. Now instead of

JESÚS CASTILLO'S
OFFICE CLEANING SERVICE
(559) 555-1232

it reads:

JESÚS CASTILLO E HIJO
TESOROS DE EL SALVADOR
(559) 555-1232

Jesús Castillo and Son. Treasures from El Salvador.

The next time I roll the van into the flea market, I receive many compliments from Carmen and Jesús' other friends.

Mom returns home from El Salvador alone, with a thin gold band on her left fourth finger and a new name—Marta Castillo. Now her last name is the same as America's instead of mine and Jojo's. It must be weird to get your name suddenly changed, but women go through it all the time. Mom looks tired but happy. A kind of calm shines in her face, lit from within. It's a kind of strength—resolve to get Jesús back. Still there's more red tape. He has to prove to the U.S. government that he has a place to stay and work to do. A guy married to one of Mom's cousins assures him of a job in a local frozen foods processing plant if he can attain a guest worker visa, so Mom files some more paperwork.

My final exams are coming up, and I have to study hard. Now I'm sure I want to go to college, and I even know my major: business! My booth at the flea market is making bank! Our kitchen table becomes a study table for all of us. A big surprise is that Jojo liked all that marching around crap at boot camp. He wants to do all his schoolwork and stay out of trouble so that the army will take him after he graduates from high school. Mom has just started up another session of nursing school, and America is reading all the Little House on the Prairie books straight through. We look forward to the day Jesús can join us at the table to study for his citizenship test. He has to know the answers to one hundred questions about the U.S. in English.

What are the thirteen original states? Which constitutional amendments grant voting rights? Who is the Chief Justice of the Supreme Court? I send him the questions in e-mails and help him understand the answers. I just learned a lot of this stuff from Ms. Becker, but it's easy to forget. I bet a lot of adults who were born in this country couldn't pass this test.

Jesús and Mom were married in a civil ceremony in El Salvador, but he wants them to have a church wedding when he gets back to Goldhurst. One of Mom's friends at the clinic insists that she borrow her daughter's wedding dress, even though Mom protests that she doesn't know when she'll get to use it. It hangs from the knob of a cupboard high above her closet, so the long white train doesn't touch the floor. There it waits and waits like a silent, determined person who refuses to be ignored. Mom and America entertain themselves by making wedding plans. America is going to be the flower girl, Jojo will be an usher, and Jesús has given me the best part of all: *el padrino de boda*, best man.

Now I know why Mom is working so hard to get Jesús back. Not because he's America's dad. Not because she thinks Jojo and me need a role model. Not because she can't find anyone else better. It's because she loves him. I think someday I'll find someone who's right for me, too.

Someday.

Chapter Twenty-eight

It's not easy letting go of someone you love. Even when you know deep in your brain she's all wrong for you, your heart still wants her.

I catch myself staring off into space, thinking about hugging, kissing, holding Monique.

I have imaginary conversations with her, like I used to with my dad. I ask her if she really ever loved me or cared about me, if she misses me now. Monique answers my questions the way I wish she would, so that after a while I know the Monique I'm imagining is far different from the real one. I want to ask her about the last day we were together, too. Does she know how really messed up her plan with America was? Is she sorry or ashamed? These thoughts go around and around in my head, and I try to forget about them.

On a few desperate, hot summer nights, I can't resist the compulsion to drive by her house. One time she even caught me and texted me, "That was weird." I'm so embarrassed I lay off for a couple of weeks.

When I dare to return, her house, like many others in that subdivision, stands empty, foreclosed by the bank. The weathered NO DOWN PAYMENT! SUBPRIME LOANS billboard lurches in the summer breeze.

One blazing hot Saturday afternoon, when I'm standing in front of my booth, hawking the rainbow-colored knit caps on a close-out sale, a couple approaches me. The girl lifts a cap off my hand. I have to raise my chin to peer out from under my wide-brimmed straw hat to see her face.

"I figure you owe me this," says Monique. She's as beautiful as ever, wearing the same bright yellow halter dress and gold flip-flops I saw her in last.

"Sure, take it," I say above the thundering of my heartbeat in my ears. "We got plenty." I think of the time last fall when I was humiliated that she might see me as a vendor at the flea market, but now I'm proud of my business.

She nods toward the guy she's with. He looks a lot like Luke Jefferson—smoking, brawny, blond—but he's about eight or ten years older than her. "This is Pete," she says.

He nods to me.

I nod back.

We don't have anything more to say to each other. She hugs me good-bye. With my wares draped across my arms and hands, I imagine it feels sort of like hugging a hat rack, but Monique just has to get her hugs in, one way or the other.

As she and her latest boyfriend saunter away, she stops at the churro booth and asks him to buy her one.

"No way, bitch. You're fat enough."

"You don't call me fat, you bastard."

The guy tries to hustle her along, but Monique resists, pulling in the opposite direction. He loses his grip on her hand, and she falls backward. She sits down hard on the burning asphalt, her skirt raised up revealing bare thighs, her red angry mouth screaming a string of obscenities.

I look away. Something stirs within me and wells up. It's like that surge of strength I feel in a wrestling match, when I know I'm going to win. A weight lifts from my chest like I'm throwing off an opponent, and I feel free.